# CHANGE YOUR MIND, CHANGE YOUR BODY

## ALSO BY SUZY PRUDDEN

*MetaFitness*, with Joan Meijer-Hirschland

*Suzy Prudden's Exercise Program for Young Children*

*Starting Right: Suzy Prudden's Fitness Program for Children*, with Joan Meijer-Hirschland

*Suzy Prudden's Pregnancy & Back-to-Shape Exercise Program*, with Jeffrey Sussman

*Suzy Prudden's Spot Reducing Program*, with Jeffrey Sussman

# CHANGE YOUR MIND, CHANGE YOUR BODY'

**SUZY PRUDDEN'S          21-DAY METAFITNESS PROGRAM**

# SUZY PRUDDEN
## AND JOAN MEIJER-HIRSCHLAND

### HarperSanFrancisco
*A Division of* HarperCollins*Publishers*

The authors gratefully acknowledge L.A. Gear, Fashions by Gilda, and Lesley Meyers of Allen Edwards Salon for their generous donations.

FIRST EDITION

**Library of Congress Cataloging-in-Publication Data**

Prudden, Suzy.
    Change your mind, change your body: Suzy Prudden's 21-day metafitness program / Suzy Prudden, Joan Meijer-Hirschland. — 1st ed.
       p.    cm.
    ISBN 0–06–250705–2 (alk. paper)
    1. Mind and body.  2. Physical fitness—Psychological aspects.  3. Affirmations.
I. Meijer-Hirschland, Joan.  II. Title.
BF161.P77   1992
613.2'5'019—dc20                           91-55326
                                                      CIP

92  93  94  95  96  CWI  10  9  8  7  6  5  4  3  2  1

This edition is printed on acid-free paper that meets the American National Standards Institute Z39.48 Standard.

The names of all the people in this book have been changed to protect client privacy and confidentiality. In many cases I have combined stories so that no friend or client will be recognizable.

The reader is strongly advised to consult with a qualified physician before embarking on any new regimen of diet or exercise.

*To Jonathan Goldhill,*
*my true friend.*
*You made me very happy.*

Suzy Prudden

*To my daughter*
*Jacqueline C. Meijer*
*who truly changed my mind*
*about my body.*

Joan Meijer-Hirschland

# Contents

# Acknowledgments

This has been a year of extremes. At times I have felt like a very small rowboat in a very large and tumultuous sea. It has been my friends and family who have consistently loved and supported me unconditionally that has kept me afloat and helped me get to calmer seas and eventually land.

Special thanks to Armand and Shannon Lee Taylor for showing me the way to go inside, experience my own quiet beauty, and bring it out softly so that I can now be quiet inside even in the midst of chaos. And to Brooks Barton, Michael Barcley, Raphael Bertolus, Francesca DiFranco, and Dori Glover, traveling together on the magic carpet of laughter, love, and self-discovery. It has been an exciting and provoking journey of enlightenment and heart-felt glee.

Thanks to those special friends who have been there for me during this year of chaos, confusion, breakdown, and breakthrough. Helaine Harris, Lynn Stewart, Cherie Carter-Scott, and Sharon Huffman, Hyla Cass, Jenny Collins, Nan Fuchs, Kathy Bradley, Sharon Lindsey, Alice March, Diana Barth, Greg and Gail Hoag, Jonathan Goldhill, David Field, David Katzin, and Andy Behrman.

To my agent and dear friend Sue Herner: Your laughter and your love fill me with delight. Supportive and kind, always there, integrous and honorable; you are a dear and trusted friend.

To my editor, Mark Salzwedel: You got me through some "interesting" and quite challenging times. Always there for me—rooting, inspiring, helping to make it all possible.

To Ellie Albeck and Al Biglar at The Printing Palace in Santa Monica—thanks for being there, for doing such good work, and for caring.

To my friend Keith Buckler, for his honesty, truth, and the honoring of friendship; for consistently making me laugh, and for always being there, even when he isn't.

To Dori (Glover) Galka and Alan Galka, who have become family: There are no words that can fully express the preciousness of our friendship.

To my aunt and uncle, Herb and Ethel Hirschland: Always there for me with love and support, know you too are loved.

As always to Rita Silverman, my dearest friend, whose vision is clear and whose heart is pure, and whom I dearly love.

And to Charlotte Williams, Carl Powell, Kris and Gigi Kory, Frank Butterfield, and Mikki Williams: You have made my reentry into the field I put aside eight years ago fun and exciting, warm and friendly. I look forward to dancing with you for a long time.

To Phyllis Pilgram at Rancho La Puerta, a woman of strength and beauty, humor and delight: It is your willingness to allow, and your sense of adventure as to the possibility in every moment, that gave me the space to create new work and to regain the love of teaching I lost eight years ago.

To Beverly Elliott, Coco Fells, and Lynda Kuebler of Canyon Ranch, who welcomed me with open minds as I taught new forms, raised eyebrows, and changed lives. Some of it worked and some of it didn't— we dared, we learned, and we grew in the process.

To Marylou Rogers-Horst of The Palms, who welcomed my expertise before I remembered I was the expert and included me in a group of experts who have since become my friends.

To Gloria Keeling, my friend and colleague, and her program Strong, Stretched and Centered: Gloria, you offered me the opportunity to see what I know and taught me that which I didn't know. Your knowledge, your love, and your support are part of the program in this book. And to Stephanie Karony: You gave me weights so that I could experience them in a new way, see their benefits, and feel their power.

To Mirka Kraftsow, who taught me how to breathe: Through yoga, you touched my heart, quieted my mind, and gave me a new way of going inside.

To Shelburn Murry and Shanna Green: Two good friends in an island of time—laughter and learning—sunrises over Haleakula—aerobics before dawn—I will always hear your smiles.

To my Maui family, Joan and Alex Lessin, with whom I close my eyes and hear music to see the world from the inside out, and in so doing, discover more about myself and the journey I have chosen. To Moonjay and Kutira, only the laughter from my heart can express my love for you—three minds as one—a time to remember. And to Bruce Rifkin, windsurfing through life, more than a chapter. . . . To Izee and Antoine, my godchildren, and to Emerald Starr, who is always in my heart.

To Jim Wilson: Redwoods and raccoons, white rainbows and whispers from within, s'mores and "who's got the hot chocolate?"

Special acknowledgments to my mother, Bonnie Prudden. "Just like when we were kids" laughing under the trees, dancing with the nature spirits—your gift to me has been the fullness in your heart, your unconditional love, your knowing and understanding, my incredible body and the training and love for movement, music, beauty, and mountains you gave me, the brilliance of your mind, the wonder of it all, and the elfin smiles behind your eyes.

To my sister, Petie, with whom I have unconditional love and friendship, respect and honoring. You are the other half of this book and a fabulous writing partner. You make me laugh—a lot.

And last, but never least, to my son, Rob Sussman. You have learned you can do anything you want. You are putting yourself through college, working and studying, following your heart. Congratulations on standing for what you want, making it happen and being fully who you are. You are a true artist, Rob. I am proud you are my sun.

And to you, dear reader, your courage, your wisdom, and your beauty. You have a precious gift to give the world. May this book bring you closer to following your heart, loving yourself, and living your purpose. Dare to follow your dreams, as they become your reality.

SUZY PRUDDEN

There is never an acknowledgment without thanking my children, Peter, Richard, and Jacqueline Meijer—my strong support system. Thank you, my loving and wonderful children now on your way to making your own successful lives. It's fun being a mother and watching your lives unfold in such perfection. Hans, of course, remains my life-long friend. My mother, Bonnie Prudden, gives me more support than I could ever have asked for. What fun that we have lived long enough to become great friends. Gon and Paps and Dad hover in the background of my mind and prove that Jean-Paul Sartre knew what he was writing about. My thanks to the Vermont contingent—Sabra Field, Caz Rozonewski, Jean Robert Ashley, Suzy Hallock, Barb Lawlor, Katherine Holmes, Dee Dee Ackeroid, and Lolo Sarnoff for always being there. Special thanks to Kathi Elster and the Business Strategy Group without whom this book and a great deal more wouldn't have gotten written. Thanks to David Winkler—I really hope we do *A Christmas Carol*. Thanks to Bill Rapp who hangs in there. Thanks to Phyllis Keitlen, Tric and Trac. Special thanks to Jane Russin, Bernetta Bradley, and all my many wonderful friends at the Ford Foundation—particularly Human Resources. Thanks also to John Kuriakose. Like Suzy, I thank Sue Herner, our agent and friend, for being in our lives and for finding us Mark Salzwedel, our wonderful editor. It's such a pleasure to work with Mark and Dean and the people at Harper San Francisco. And there's always thanks to Suzy Prudden, friend, sister, confidant.

JOAN MEIJER-HIRSCHLAND

x

# Introduction

When the topic of writing a metaphysical diet and exercise book came up, I stopped for a moment and asked myself why anybody would want another diet and exercise book, even a metaphysical one. The answer is in the question: To my knowledge, there are no metaphysical diet and exercise books. There are books on diet and books on exercise, but there are no books on diet *and* exercise.

Most diet and exercise books deal with symptoms, not causes. From my point of view, eating disorders—which include overeating, anorexia, bulimia, and excessive dieting—result from something else. If you don't address the something else, you get a yo-yo effect and often disease. Most dieters experience this yo-yo effect, perhaps losing 10 pounds and gaining 11. Overzealous dieters often become ill; anorexia and bulimia have been known to be fatal; and fad diets and weight-loss drugs can cause irreparable damage. The issue is not *losing weight*, but *changing your habits*. To change your habits, you have to change your mind. And while most diet books tell you to exercise, they don't specify a program to follow. And most exercise books may tell you to eat healthily, but they don't give you a diet. *Change Your Mind, Change Your Body* does all three. It addresses ways to change the way you think about yourself, about food, and about exercise. It gives you a complete exercise program *plus* affirmations that enhance the effectiveness of the exercises as well as help you overcome any resistance you might have to exercise in general. Finally, this book teaches you how to listen to what your body wants and needs to eat, how much it wants to eat, and which foods are best suited for it at any given time. Because I understand that each person's nutritional needs are different, I offer you a sensible choice of foods from which to structure your own healthy diet.

This is a diet book for life. This is not a diet book that will teach you how to lose 10 pounds in 10 days. This is not a magic bullet. This is a

*The issue is not* losing weight, *but* changing your habits. *To change your habits, you have to change your mind.*

book for people who are tired of the yo-yo, tired of feeling frustrated, tired of feeling angry with themselves, tired of blaming themselves for something they don't seem to be able to help, tired of feeling powerless around food, tired of battling with themselves, and tired of feeling like failures. This book has real answers.

Another difference in this program is its "no gain in pain" philosophy. Most diets and many exercise programs require self-punishment, self-denial, and physical abuse. *Change Your Mind, Change Your Body* is built on reward, self-love, building self-esteem, and self-acceptance. I don't believe for a moment that you can punish yourself into having the body you want.

*Change Your Mind, Change Your Body* is a program that takes you on a journey of self-discovery. This journey can be scary at times, but you will learn that your fear has no basis in reality. *FEAR* stands for False Evidence Appearing Real. There are no monsters.

"I don't have time" is the biggest and most common excuse for not doing something for yourself. I have heard this excuse everywhere I have traveled since 1978 on 16 national and international tours.

Whenever you get to a point of discomfort in building self-esteem or in personal growth, you will mysteriously run out of time to continue the program. If you really begin to make progress, then you may forget you're even in a program and days might go by before you pick up this book again. Experts agree: One out of every 200 people who start a diet successfully completes it; 85 percent of people who sign up for exercise programs drop out before the first day. Only 3 percent of all people who start exercise programs continue for the long term. Diet and exercise are not easily accomplished parts of our lives.

As I began to develop this program, I found that I had a tendency to put myself last. With every phone call, every intrusion, the needs of everyone else came first. Not until I put myself first was I able to make true progress. The way I did this was by making appointments with myself as if I were someone else. I know how to keep appointments with other people, and now I know how to keep appointments with myself.

Make a commitment *right now* to finish this program. Acknowledge *right now* that it will be a challenge. And know *right now* that if you finish this program, you can be certain that you will have changed not only your eating and exercise habits, but also your body and your life.

## WHAT YOU WILL NEED

This book is a combination of workbook and journal. You will need a blank book, a notebook or some kind of journal, to supplement the space provided in the workbook sections in this book. I also use an appointment calendar and set aside specific times to do the work. And you will need a very small notebook that fits in a purse or a pocket for writing down what you eat at every meal and how your body feels after you have finished.

I also have found it helpful to work with a friend. Although you may not want to share all the revelations you uncover about yourself, using a friend for support can help keep you focused on your purpose.

The journey you are about to take is both fun and exciting. You are about to discover wonderful things about the most important person in your life. You are about to heal your relationship with the house you live in. Roll up your sleeves and have a good time.

# The World as We Understand It Is Completely Backward

*I think, therefore I am.*

René Descartes

I discovered the backward nature of the world during my 10-year pursuit of answers that were supposed to "straighten out" my life. Over those years, I learned that all the little rules and all the old beliefs—that whole foundation I had so carefully developed as an underpinning to explain how life worked—didn't serve me. Those rules didn't serve me because they never answered my questions. They didn't answer my questions because they were totally backward. These were not answers at all; these rules and beliefs were conclusions based on a whole cluster of faulty premises. If your foundation is wrong, how can the rest of you be right?

Some of the rules and beliefs I used to live by were:

- You have to diet to be thin.
- "If you love me, you'll eat everything I cooked for you."
- You must perform even if you are in pain.
- There is never enough.
- Fat people are lazy.
- Thin is better, emaciated is best.
- Chocolate gives you energy.
- You have to finish everything on your plate.

- Sex is dirty. Save it for the one you love.
- Fat is ugly.
- Life is hard.
- Your behavior reflects on your parents and your partner, and their behavior reflects on you.
- You have to earn love.
- Everyone's out to get you.
- You're never good enough, pretty enough, smart enough, rich enough . . .

That's enough.

As I read over the list, I see again that those are pretty depressing rules to live by. Are any of them yours? If they are, would you like to live by different rules? You can. The good news is that none of these rules are real. You made them up, or someone else made them up and you believed them. And you can make up different rules to live by if these don't suit you.

As I look over the first 37 years of my life, I find they were not very much fun. Oh yes, I made a lot of money, I had two homes, I traveled extensively (first class), I was a published author with an ever-increasing number of books to my credit, I was a television personality, I was recognized on the street, in airports, restaurants, clubs . . . , but I wasn't happy.

Although I had all the accoutrements of fame and fortune, I worked an 18-hour day seven days a week, so I was constantly exhausted, I was thin from bulimia, and I was in constant physical pain (pain pills masked it for years; I became addicted to them).

Even worse than the pain and exhaustion, I never *felt* successful. No matter how well I performed, no matter how much money I made, no matter how much I did, I never felt good enough, beautiful enough, smart enough, thin enough, or rich enough. *I* was never enough.

The point is, if you believe you are not enough, then you never *will* be enough.

## UNDERLYING BELIEFS

Let me state this another way, because it's the core concept of this book. *Thought is creative. What you believe to be true* is *true.* So how and where does all the pain and misery begin? It begins in childhood. Childhood is the foundation for the rest of our lives. The rules, the regulations, the interpretation of events all come from childhood and the child's unformed and literal mind.

That's not a particularly radical insight. Everyone knows that childhood affects adult life in some way. What is not so commonly known is that it is not so much what *happened* in childhood that affects adult life, but what is *believed to have happened.* The entire belief system of an adult is based on a small child's interpretation of events.

*What is not so commonly known is that it is not so much what* happened *in childhood that affects adult life, but what is* believed to have happened.

6

Some years ago, my sister Joan and I were sharing memories about our childhood when I jokingly asked her, "Are you sure we come from the same family?" Our recollections of the same events and experiences are entirely different. Joan hated sports as a child, and I loved them. Joan believed that what she was forced to do—the operational word is *forced*—was dangerous, difficult, life-threatening, and miserable. I believed that the opportunities I was offered—the operational word is *opportunities*—were dangerous, difficult, life-threatening—*and* fun, exciting, exhilarating, and challenging.

For years, Joan believed that our mother, Bonnie Prudden, the nation's foremost fitness authority and sports enthusiast, didn't like her, because Mother continually forced her to do the things she hated. I, on the other hand, believed our mother was my best friend, because she taught me how to do all the things I loved. Our mother offered us the same things. It was the way we understood and received them that made the difference.

As our conversation began to really dig into our experiences, Joan discovered that it wasn't so much that she didn't enjoy the sports, but that she felt she was never very good at them. (She was my role model; I thought she was terrific!) I, on the other hand, believed that I was a masterly athlete. We now think the breakdown in Joan's perception occurred because Mother's way of teaching was to use "going to the next level" as the reward for achievement. I interpreted that as our mother intended: as recognition for my prowess. But because I was always the smallest, there was always an element of my not being enough in everything I did. Joan, however, found that whenever she got comfortable, she was pushed to the next level, so she never felt good enough.

Joan's underlying life belief, which was formed very early in childhood, is that she's not good enough. That's a very common belief. It began early, was reinforced in sports, and then manifested itself in every single aspect of her life. And it is untrue. It has no basis in reality, yet it still colors everything.

My own underlying belief is that I am not enough. Oh, I know I'm *good* enough. *I* am just not *enough*.

How did we uncover these beliefs? Joan had memories to help her discover her underlying core belief, but I didn't remember anything that would uncover mine. Rather than wait until the memories came, I used a different tactic. I uncovered my underlying belief by looking closely at the repeating patterns of my life as it is now, the results of my beliefs.

When I visit friends, I never arrive empty-handed. Very often, *I* pay for dinner. If I need or want something from someone, I am sure that I return something even better than what I receive. I very often teach a class past the allotted time. When I go shopping, I often buy more than I need so that I always have the right clothes, enough food in the house should company drop in, and gifts on hand just in case I need to give something to someone. I travel with my computer, three suitcases, and several boxes of books. I do all these things so that no one will discover that *I* am not enough.

There are several clues to discovering your underlying belief. One is the results in your life. If you are constantly failing, it may be that you don't feel good enough to succeed. If you are a superachiever, it may be that you have never felt good enough and have overcompensated. If your underlying belief is that you are not enough, you will always try to fill the space that *you* ought to occupy with *things*.

## EXERCISE

Take a moment to look at what you believe about yourself. List five behavior patterns that you repeat constantly.

## Example

In the past, Joan always sabotaged her business and her creative ideas just when it looked as if they might work. If Joan didn't do it, then life did it. The result was the same: She was not good enough.

Your turn: _____

_____

_____

_____

_____

(If you need more space, use your journal.)

What did you notice in the exercise you just completed? Did you see consistencies? Did you see inconsistencies? A kiwi and a banana are both fruit; don't be misled by superficial differences in the things that are troubling you. Look for commonality.

Perhaps you are now wondering why you have to learn about underlying beliefs in a diet book. I am assuming that, like me, you have tried many diets and they didn't work. I maintain that it is the underlying belief, not the diet, that keeps the diet from working.

Looking at underlying beliefs is only the first step in identifying the factors that keep you from making the changes you want to make. During the 21-Day Program, you will have many opportunities to explore your belief system and its effects on your body.

The underlying belief system—"not good enough" in Joan's case and "not enough" in my case—develops in childhood. It is formed by the conclusions the child draws from his or her observations of life. Many life-ruling decisions are made in childhood. One of the biggest, and most debilitating, of these decisions is that the child "doesn't know anything."

The child is a sensory being. It is completely in tune with its own body. And the first thing it has to learn to do is override that body.

*I maintain that it is the underlying belief, not the diet, that keeps the diet from working.*

8

# THE VARIOUS FORMS OF FORCE-FEEDING

In every lecture I give, I always ask the group, "How many here belonged to the 'clean-plate club' as children?" There is usually a pause as the group grasps what I have asked, and then 98 percent of the people in the room raise their hands. Then I ask, "How many of you are still finishing everything on your plate?" A few hands go down, but most stay up.

Can *you* remember having to eat everything on your plate?

Joan and I can both recall one weekend morning when our parents insisted that Joan finish her cold, congealed fried eggs. Poor Joan had to sit at the table for what seemed like hours. She would gag every time she put a forkful in her mouth. Even though Joan was a "good little girl," she couldn't finish the eggs. She also couldn't throw them out, because she couldn't disobey or lie. We figured she would have to sit there all day. I thought it was the meanest, dumbest thing in the world.

Super little sister to the rescue. *I* threw out the eggs. And when Mother, looking furious, accused Joan of throwing them out, I jumped in with "No she didn't!" And, for once, Joan didn't say, "Suzy did it."

Can you remember any uncomfortable incidents that occurred around food in your childhood? _____

_____

_____

The patterns set up in childhood still affect you.

I used to save the favorite part of my meal for last. I was usually full by the time I had to eat it, but it was easier to eat something I liked when I was full. I still find myself occasionally saving the choice bits. The repercussions for me were very serious. To gain a measure of control over my intake, I learned to throw up. Bulimia ruled my life off and on for 25 years.

We are taught to override our bodies not only with regard to stuffing, but also with regard to taste. "Eat your spinach—it's good for you" is an "override" if you don't like spinach. In overriding our natural inclinations about taste, we rob ourselves of one of our greatest pleasures and one of our best defenses against accidental poisoning. Sometimes if you don't like something, there's a good reason.

When he was a boy, my son wouldn't eat tomatoes. He hated them. Tomatoes became a red flag at the dinner table. My husband was certain that Rob was being belligerent. Rob was certain that his father was mean. I quickly learned never to put tomatoes on the table. One night in a restaurant they appeared, and they appeared on Robby's plate. I guess we all saw them at the same moment. Jeffrey immediately focused all his attention on making sure Rob ate the tomatoes. Rob immediately set about eating everything *but* . . . and I started praying we'd survive the meal without a public scene. We didn't. At one point, Jeff actually shoved a piece of tomato into Rob's mouth, and Rob simply vomited all over the table.

Force-feeding can take more subtle forms. Joan and I had a grandmother who was a fabulous cook. She always made our favorite foods when we went to visit her—*all* our favorite foods. The good news was that we loved our grandparents, and dinner at Gon and Pap's was always a special occasion. The bad news was that we had to eat *all* of it. "What? You don't want dessert? I made meringue with ice cream and strawberries, 'specially for you. I thought it was your favorite." Then our grandfather would chime in, "Gonny spent all afternoon in the kitchen preparing this dinner just for you." We ate it. We were good little girls. And we learned to override our body messages. We learned to press on even when our bodies were uncomfortable. We learned to eat fast so that our bodies wouldn't send us "full" messages before we'd finished everything. Both Joan and I still eat fast and press on.

*Most people with weight problems were force-fed in some way as children.*

Most people with weight problems were force-fed in some way as children. Food was the focus of every meal, and the food was in control. In a strange way, those little children are still being force-fed. This is the time to remember what you were forced to eat as a child, and whether you were made to finish everything on your plate.

Take a moment to look at your eating habits now.

- Do you finish everything on your plate?
- When was the last time you sent something back in a restaurant because it wasn't what you wanted?
- Have you been around someone who sent something back? What was your reaction?
- When was the last time you ate something simply because you had paid for it?
- Do you find yourself doing unto your children as was done unto you? (If so, don't worry about it. You won't be doing it after you finish this book.)

## REASONS FOR EATING

Guilt is one reason you override your body and eat too much, or eat the foods you don't like. What are some of the others?

- Eating for comfort.
- Eating because you like the taste of the food.
- Eating as a reward (for good behavior).
- Eating because of the starving children in . . .
- Eating because someone else is paying for it.
- Eating because you're on vacation.

- Eating because you're in a new and different place and you may never get this opportunity again.
- Eating because it's good for you.
- Eating because you need the energy.
- Eating because you're bored.
- Eating because you're watching TV.
- Eating because you're at an event.
- Eating because you might be hungry later.
- Eating because it's time.
- Eating because you're bigger and need more food.
- Eating because you're smaller and have to catch up.
- Eating because you exercised hard or because you're going to.
- Eating because you're about to go on a diet.
- Eating because you've just been on a diet and now it's okay.
- Eating because you're angry.
- Eating because you're sad.
- Eating because it's paid for.
- Eating because it's there.
- Eating because it's "the best restaurant in town."
- Eating because it'll go to waste.

Did you notice that none of these reasons for eating has anything to do with actual hunger?

Eating too much is one side of the pendulum swing of overriding your body; starving yourself is the other. Have you ever been on a strict diet? Have you ever consumed so few calories that you felt as if you wanted to eat the bed when you got into it at night? Sure, the weight fell off, but you probably traumatized and confused your body in the process. And how long did it take before the weight went back on?

The body needs food to function. Like gasoline in a car, give it too much and it will spill over (fat is the equivalent of spillage); give it too little and it won't run (you become confused and irritable). A car is actually pretty healthy. If you feed it too much, the gas doesn't turn to cellulite in the fenders. If you feed it too little, it doesn't cannibalize its vital tissue. The human body will do anything to keep running. A car will simply stop.

The old saying "You are what you eat" has some basis in truth. If you eat too much, the body has to store the excess, because of the primitive "feast-or-famine" conditions it used to know. It will store excess food as fat, anywhere it can: around the heart, in the blood vessels, in the thighs. If you eat too little, the body simply devours itself; it starts with fat and goes through tissue.

The quality of the food eaten, not just the amount, determines whether you are eating too much or too little. By *quality*, I mean how well the body is able to utilize it. Simply stated, if you eat junk, the body doesn't get fed. Empty calories are just that: They require energy to burn and give nothing in return. Ever wonder why you can't think properly when you're on a diet or on a binge?

I can't promise that you will ever have complete control over any of this stuff. What I can promise is that, by the end of my 21-Day Program, you will be aware of what's going on and be able to choose to stop if you want. Sometimes you will and sometimes you won't. Awareness is the key.

*Awareness is the key.*

## OVERRIDING THE BODY

Eating is not the only area in which we override our bodies. Most people have learned to press on in all parts of their lives regardless of how they feel. We learn early in childhood that our bodies don't count, so most of us don't pay attention to what our bodies tell us when it comes to being tired, injured, or ill. It's almost as if we have to be totally knocked off our feet before we'll pay attention.

Ask yourself these questions:

- Do you stay up late when you're tired, because it's not *time* to go to sleep?
- Do you go to work even when you're sick?
- Do you exercise to the point of pain?
- Do you push yourself to the point of exhaustion just before vacation?
- Do you do exercises you hate because someone told you they were "good for you"?
- Do you do *anything* you hate because it's good for you?

You've probably been overriding your body for so long and in so many ways that you've actually developed an adversarial relationship with it. You probably act as if you think your body is against you when, in actuality, it is the house you live in and, as such, is an integral part of you. It's almost as if you feel that you and your body are separate entities, as if you believe that if you ignore illness, injury, and exhaustion they will simply go away. Not so. Illness, injury, and exhaustion will go away only if you pay attention to their signals and take care of them promptly.

Just as my son Rob wasn't being belligerent when he didn't want to eat tomatoes, your body isn't being belligerent when it becomes full or tired. It's just letting you know that it needs to stop eating, to eat different foods, or to rest awhile.

## LOVE YOURSELF FIRST

There's another message in overriding your body: the hidden agenda. Constantly overriding your body suggests that you believe effort, struggle, pain, deprivation, self-denial, and discomfort constitute, in some strange way, the accepted way of being. Taken one step further, it's as if they have become good for you. And this message relates not just to your body, but carries over into every other aspect of your life. If you don't have a good relationship with your own body, you will allow yourself to be uncomfortable at work, in relationships, and with your family. If you hurt *yourself*, you will allow others to hurt you.

The Bible says to do unto others as you would have done unto you. The way that is usually interpreted is, Be nice to people so that they'll be nice to you. I have never found that to work. I think we have it backward. My interpretation of that phrase is closer to that of Polonius in *Hamlet:*

This above all: To thine own self be true,
And it must follow, as the night the day,
Thou canst not then be false to any man.

Some years ago, Joan attended a workshop called "The Loving Relationships Training." One of the exercises was to write "a completion letter to your parents." Joan thought the completion letter to our mother would be very easy and very long. After about a page and a half of complaint, she suddenly realized that the things she was complaining about with respect to Mother were the same things she always heard Mother complaining about to her. She wrote the following letter:

Dear Mother,

I've been asked to write a "completion" letter to you. In the process of writing the letter I have discovered that the thing I most want from you is the thing I can't give you: unconditional love. I think when I can love you unconditionally, you'll be able to love me the same way. First, I have to learn to love myself unconditionally. I do love you very much.

The purpose of this book is to help you learn to love and accept yourself unconditionally, because the key to change is unconditional self-acceptance. If you've tried every diet there is, as most of us have, if you've tried overexercising and undereating, if you still have a weight problem, then you know you can't deal with it through pain and deprivation. The only other alternative is to deal with it through self-love.

Let me show you how that works. If you constantly try to change yourself by making yourself wrong and depriving yourself, eventually you're going to have to rebel. One way to rebel is by rewarding or comforting yourself with food. If, on the other hand, you treat yourself well—and that means having others treat you well, too—if you never set up any areas for rebellion, you never have to overeat. You never have to reward yourself or punish yourself with food. Food does not become a substitute for something else.

In the next 21 days, you will uncover your negative beliefs about yourself and your life and turn them around. You'll begin to see how wonderful you are now, just the way you are, with all your lovable and (supposedly) unlovable parts. "The world as we understand it is completely backward." That simply means we have been taught to make ourselves better by making ourselves wrong. What I will share with you is how to make yourself better by making yourself right. Self-acceptance is the first step to change, and awareness is the key.

# How MetaFitness Works

*In the beginning was the Word . . . and the Word was made flesh. . .*

John 1:1, 1:14

**M**etaFitness is a process of using positive thought, visual images, diet, and exercise to achieve positive results. It is based on the principle that thought is creative. You can make the life and body you want by creating the thoughts you want. Many of you are ruled by the thoughts you don't want, which create the life and body you don't want.

To understand MetaFitness, you need to understand the subconscious mind. Though deeply hidden, it colors every aspect of your life. It's always working, but you don't always know what it's thinking. Indeed, the only way to figure out what it's thinking is to look at the results it helps produce.

## YOUR SUBCONSCIOUS MIND AT WORK

Your subconscious mind is strictly literal. It has no sense of humor, no ability to understand sarcasm or translate tones of voice. It's like a computer: What you put into it, you get out of it (garbage in, garbage out). The kicker is, you don't know what you put into it.

Your subconscious mind operates on the premises "What you focus on expands" and "Thought is creative: What you believe to be true becomes true for you." If you constantly repeat that you are fat, the subconscious mind doesn't hear that as a negative judgment; it doesn't understand that you may not want to be fat. It is very obliging: It wants to prove you right. So it will either help you gain weight so that you get to be right about being fat, or it will cause you to *see* yourself as fat, regardless of the reality, which can develop into anorexia.

When I first heard this concept I rejected it totally. It seemed to me that my teachers were saying I was guilty of creating all the awful things that were going on in my life and with my body. But since no other concept had worked, I figured I had nothing to lose by trying to use this one. I began to look at what was happening in my life as planned results rather than random chaos. And I found that accepting the premise that I create my life and my body with my thoughts, even thoughts of which I am unaware, meant that I no longer saw myself as a victim of uncontrollable outside events. I could identify what I was thinking, and I could change my mind. I became empowered.

*What if what you want is what you've got?*

If you are like most people who are overweight, you believe that you don't have what you want. You believe that what you want is to be thin. But what if you're wrong? What if you have it backward? What if overweight is what you *subconsciously* really want? What if subconsciously you feel safe being overweight? What if subconsciously you feel in control being overweight? What if subconsciously you feel powerful being overweight? What if what you want is what you've got?

Your subconscious mind is the power behind the throne. What you've got is what your subconscious mind wants. In order to make changes in your body, you have to deal with the subconscious mind. You have to accept that what you've got *is* what you want and then begin changing your mind. The 21-Day Program is designed to help you change your mind.

MetaFitness deals with the underlying thoughts that rule your life: the cause. MetaFitness reprograms that computer (your subconscious mind) so that you can go forward and make the changes you want to make. Other plans don't usually work over the long haul because they deal with the *results* of the computer programming, rather than with the program itself. Other plans work with masking the symptoms; MetaFitness works with healing the disease. If you deal with the symptoms and not with the cause, the symptoms will recur.

The subconscious mind has no picture for the word *no* in any of its variations: *don't, won't, shouldn't, couldn't, can't.* For example, "Don't think of a purple parrot." Is the purple parrot you just thought of at this moment sitting in a tree or in a cage? Not that it matters; the purpose of that exercise was to illustrate how the subconscious mind works: Tell it "don't" and it does.

Most diets tell you "don't," so that you won't, but because the subconscious mind can't hear *n't,* you do it anyway. Let's look at some examples. How many times have you promised yourself *not* to gain weight over the holidays? How many times have you promised yourself *not* to eat sugar? How many times have you said you *won't* cheat on your diet? How many times have you used the words *don't* or *won't,* only to find yourself doing? It's a simple concept that can basically change your life when you pay attention to it.

## DIETS AS PUNISHMENT

Most other diets make you wrong for being overweight; that's the premise of a diet. That's why the word *diet* has such hideous connotations to most people. *Diet* is equated with self-loathing and deprivation. Self-loathing and deprivation are not sufficient motivations for long-term change. Implicit in self-loathing and deprivation is the concept of punishment, and you will punish yourself with a diet only so long before you stop.

As soon as you stop punishing and depriving yourself with the diet, the things we talked about in Chapter 1 under "Reasons for Eating" kick in: rewarding yourself for having dieted, needing energy, now it's okay to go back to "normal," I can always lose it again.

Because diets deal with deprivation, feelings of self-loathing, and punishment, the creators of diets have developed any number of silver bullets, magic time frames, and quick fixes. Since most people hate diets, they want to be on one for the shortest period of time possible. They also want to see instant results. The creators of diets know this, so they build speed into their regimens rather than lasting results. Speed is the only thing they can offer. (One of the notable exceptions here is Weight Watchers, which actually offers reprogramming of your eating habits.)

The other thing most conventional diets offer is the illusion of control. If every piece of food is weighed, measured, or prepared for you, you never have to take responsibility for controlling your eating except when you stop dieting, and then it's right back to the way you were eating before—and often more so.

A useful analogy can be found in medicine. It is well known that if a medical condition develops rapidly, it must be treated rapidly; if it develops slowly, it can be treated slowly. There's no such thing as instant weight gain.

## WHY METAFITNESS WORKS

The major difference between MetaFitness and conventional diets is that MetaFitness deals with long-term solutions to long-term problems. It took years to cement those hidden beliefs in your subconscious mind. In most cases it takes a while to figure out where the subconscious is misfiring. MetaFitness takes time, but it works over time. You don't have to be a yo-yo anymore.

Most diets tell you to eat certain foods in certain amounts to lose weight; they give you a generic formula without teaching you how to continue the process of eating right for the rest of your life. The 21-Day Program is not generic. It's tailored by you to your own needs. Continuing the process does not mean staying on a diet, it means knowing what foods affect your body negatively and what foods affect it positively. Journal work in the 21-Day Program will guide you to an understanding of what foods do and don't work for you. By writing down how you feel after you've eaten, exercised, sat, slept, worked, and so on, you will heighten your awareness of how your body responds to a variety of stimuli. Your own body will become the guide that will tell you what to eat, how much sleep you need, what makes you tense, how to release that tension, and what is toxic to your body in the areas of pollution, noise, odor, emotion, thoughts, people, and general living conditions. The next step, of course, is honoring what the body tells you and acting on it, but that's another issue.

MetaFitness works because it deals with cause, not symptom. It deals with control, not the illusion of control. It focuses on self-appreciation, not self-loathing. It focuses on reward, not deprivation. It makes you right, not wrong. It works to change subconscious thinking and allows positive results.

## YOUR BODY IS A MESSAGE MACHINE

Chapter 1 discussed how we were taught to override our bodies when we were children. Basically, we learned how to ignore what our bodies have to say to us. Your body knows all kinds of things. It has visceral reactions to people you don't like, it virtually throbs when you're attracted to someone, it warns you of danger and relaxes in safety. There are many body messages you might have become aware of now that we're talking about them; there are many subtle ones you may have to relearn to hear. MetaFitness teaches you how to listen to your body—to recognize its signals and to interpret what they mean.

How many times have you looked back over something that went wrong and realized you had known beforehand that it would? So many people have told me, "If I had just listened to my intuition." Intuition and subtle body signals are the same thing.

The messages your body sends you are signals of what's going on in your life. Your body knows long before your conscious mind. It has a language and a voice of its own. It speaks in a crawling of the flesh, a tightening of the neck, a contraction of the stomach; it speaks in weight gain and weight loss. The trick is to train yourself to listen to it and to understand it before it has to start screaming. Illness, injury, spasm, excessive weight gain or loss are the body's ways of screaming that something isn't right in your life.

In her book *You Can Heal Your Life*, Louise L. Hay talks about what each part of the body represents in your life. For example: Your shoulders represent your ability to carry your experiences of life. If you have pain in your shoulders, you may be carrying your experiences as burdens. To release the pain you must release the burdens.

Ultimately, to create change in your body you have to understand what it's telling you and then you have to follow through. This may seem strange at first; you may ask, "How can my body tell me I'm carrying my life experiences as burdens?" For the moment, take it on faith and begin to notice what's going on in your life when your body feels uncomfortable.

*MetaFitness works because it deals with cause, not symptom.*

## YOUR BODY NEEDS BALANCE

The body operates in a polar manner. When food goes into the stomach, it is broken down by acid. As soon as it hits the small intestine, the acid is neutralized by alkali. Acid and alkali are chemical opposites, but they work together to process the food you eat. Likewise, muscles work in opposition. Muscles do only two things: They tighten and relax. Everything you do physically is accomplished by muscles tightening and relaxing. Because the body is a polar machine, it needs balance. Too much contracting of a muscle will cause spasm, too little sleep will cause exhaustion, too much tension can result in any number of major medical conditions, too much food results in becoming overweight.

In all the conditions listed above we see cause and effect at work: Too much of something has a result. But the cause of the cause has not yet been addressed. Certainly, an overcontracting muscle will result in spasm, but what's causing the overcontraction? Too little sleep will definitely result in exhaustion, but what's causing the sleeplessness? Too much tension can give you an ulcer or high blood pressure, but what are the sources of tension and how do you deal with them? Too much food definitely results in overweight, but what is stimulating the need for too much food, and how can you retrain your body to achieve balance?

What is balance, anyway? It is the high state of perfection in your body when everything is working well. Its most fundamental form as applied to food is: You eat when you're hungry, you stop when you're full. You never eat to excess or discomfort, you never delay gratification, you never eat for any reason other than hunger. If you apply this same concept to other spheres of life—work, play, rest, and exercise—you'll find that most people don't lead very balanced lives. Every area of your life affects the other areas. If you are out of balance in one area, you'll probably see the results in many others.

The 21-Day Program should heighten your awareness of balance, and highlight the areas where you are out of balance. Once you are aware, you can choose to change.

## YOUR BODY IS PHYSICAL

In his best-selling book *The Third Wave*, Alvin Toffler discusses the role of the public school in fostering the Industrial Revolution. As he describes it, schools were designed to train farmers, who were very much in tune with the balance of nature and their own bodies, how to sit for long periods of time so that they could work in factories. Basically, they were taught to override everything they knew. They had to forget that they were physical entities.

Today's society has carried this override to illogical extremes. We think nothing of sitting for days at a time, or, conversely, exercising our bodies to the point of injury. Unfortunately, overriding, abuse, pain, and deprivation have become synonymous with good behavior. In today's society we are judged by our ability to withstand pain. The more pain and abuse you can take (cheerfully), the better you are considered to be. You might want to change that.

## THERE IS NO GAIN IN PAIN

Sitting too much, exercising to the point of injury, withstanding verbal and emotional abuse, not getting enough sleep, working too hard, playing too little are all considered optimum modes of good behavior—that's what people do to get ahead. All these modes of behavior are variations on the theme of enduring pain. Even as the virtues of a painful existence continue to be extolled, we are experiencing a surge of stress-related illnesses in this country, many of which are lifestyle-related. Until we heal our lifestyle, we risk major disease. We have to learn that there is no gain in pain and adjust our lives accordingly.

If you are overweight, if you are experiencing pain, if you are experiencing tension, fatigue, frequent colds or flu, if you don't feel well, your body is trying to tell you something. Listening to the body is the first step in overcoming many major health problems. Your body will teach you how to live well if you listen to it.

**CHAPTER**

**3**

# Mind Chatter

*Our life is what our thoughts make it.*

Marcus Aurelius
*Meditations*

**W**hether you know it or not, your mind talks all the time. It chatters nonstop. Very often it has conversations with itself (who else would it be talking to?). Most of the time it thinks it's more interesting than anyone else. Sometimes it interviews itself for television or solves the mystery you're reading. It constantly comments on other people's figures—at least mine does. It can make you laugh or bring you to the edge of tears, and no one else has to be in the room.

For the next couple of days, practice listening to your running thoughts. Everyone has these thoughts, but because they're so constant and so fast, not everyone hears them. It's important to become aware of these thoughts, so that you can consciously hear them—they will tell you how you regard yourself, others, and life. As I said earlier, your thoughts become your reality; what you think becomes manifest in your life. Once you discover what your thoughts are saying, you can discover what you are creating. This takes practice, patience, and time.

Probably the most important and difficult thing to learn about thoughts is that they're just thoughts. Even though they create your reality, they aren't real.

One of my favorite stories about mind chatter comes from a friend of mine in New York. She had recently moved to the city and was doing office temp work. She had landed an assignment with a bank that was supposed to be long-term, but during the first week they found that things were slow and they let her go. As she was walking home she noticed that her mind was screaming at her. "You'll never get another temp job," it said. "You'll never make enough money to pay the rent. They'll put you out on the street. You'll starve and be dirty like the homeless people. No one will ever let you take a shower again . . ."

My friend knows about mind chatter. "What are you talking about?" she asked her mind. "And what about the children?" it shouted back (her children were all grown). "We're going to the movies," she told her mind, and they did. When they came out two hours later, her mind had nothing to say, which was not necessarily a comment on the movie. The point of the story is that if my friend had not recognized the uncontrolled mind chatter for what it was, she could have spent a very uncomfortable evening, believing the things her mind was telling her. Over the long term, given runaway mind chatter, she could have created a very uncomfortable existence for herself.

In a convoluted way, mind chatter is your protector. It is the voice that worries when the boss says he wants to see you. It worries that he's going to fire you irrespective of the fact that you're doing a good job. Mind chatter is the voice that worries that there isn't enough money to get you through the month, irrespective of your bank balance. Mind chatter is the voice that keeps you eating beyond full because of the fear you may never eat again, or that whoever is serving the meal won't like you if you don't eat what she or he has cooked, or you may never have an opportunity to eat this type of food again. Mind chatter is the frightened inner you, the child who was vulnerable, at risk, powerless, and trying to be the best little child possible.

Mind chatter is your protector, your tormentor, your saboteur. You may be saying at this point, "I don't hear a little voice. People who hear little voices are crazy." The voice that's telling you you don't have a little voice *is* the little voice.

## WHAT HAS YOUR MIND BEEN SAYING TO YOU?

Now that you know that you too have a mind-chatter voice, you may want to learn how to listen to it. It's easier to hear when it's out of control, like my friend's voice that told her she'd never work again, than when it comments quietly. Background comments can go something like this:

At a party recently a friend who hadn't seen me in a while told me how great I looked. My immediate inner response was, "Yes, except for the extra ten pounds." That's a long response and it's easy to hear once you know what you're listening for.

Another response, which is not so easily heard, happened to a client. She was copying affirmations for one of my prosperity workshops from the book *Money Is My Friend* by Phil Laut. She wrote, "I can create my own, vast, personal fortune." In a quick little sarcastic whisper her mind chatter said "Sure." It was so fast and so quiet she almost missed it. But she didn't miss it, and as it turns out, believing that she can create her own fortune is a major problem area for her. She wouldn't have known it if she hadn't caught the whisper.

Mind chatter can seem very logical. Both Joan and I have experienced moments of great terror when it seemed as if things were not going to work out well in our lives, until we realized that mind chatter was doing the talking. With few exceptions, those moments when you feel most futile, most frightened, are mind-chatter moments.

*Mind chatter is the frightened inner you, the child who was vulnerable, at risk, powerless, and trying to be the best little child possible.*

It's important at this point to isolate your mind chatter and for the purposes of this book we'll use the body as its subject. Do the following "You Are Beautiful" mirror exercise. To do this exercise you will stand in front of a mirror and talk to yourself. Let your mind respond the way it normally does (you will do a great deal more of this process when you get to the 21-Day Program).

**Example**

I am standing in front of a mirror. I say to myself, "You are beautiful." My mind responds with, "Yeah, sure, except for the bags under your eyes and the fact that your pants are too tight." That's my mind chatter. To take it one step further I say, "You have a beautiful body." My mind simply sighs. That's mind chatter as well, subtle and deadly.

Your turn: Stand in front of a full-length mirror (if you don't have a full-length mirror, visit a friend, or use a plate-glass window). Look at yourself and say, "You are beautiful." Now, what did your mind say?

_____

_____

You can use this process to identify your mind chatter in everything you do. Mind chatter is the part of you that has thought it was protecting you by criticizing you negatively to make you "better," but in reality it has been holding you back.

There's another aspect of mind chatter you ought to be aware of. Mind chatter also occurs when other people express your worst thoughts about yourself. This is particularly true of body issues and most particularly true of weight. When you hear "helpful" people say "supportive" things like "You have such a beautiful face. If only you could lose 50 pounds,'" they're only supporting your worst thoughts about yourself. Their opinion isn't any more real than your mind chatter. And as with your mind chatter, you don't have to agree.

If your thoughts create your reality, then mind chatter—which is a form of thought—also helps create that reality. Other people's agreement with your mind chatter, their "helpful" negative criticism, which on some level you agree with, perpetuates your mind chatter and therefore perpetuates the reality you don't want.

## CANCELING

To combat all mind chatter, you first have to hear it. Once you've heard it, you have to cancel it. You cancel it by immediately saying, "Cancel that thought. I will replace that thought with something positive." Even if you can't come up with a positive thought at that moment, the act of canceling the negative thought will work.

You must begin policing your mind. If you want to create positive change in your life, you have to stop the negative mind chatter.

## HOW TO USE MIND CHATTER TO
## IDENTIFY WHAT'S HOLDING YOU BACK

Listen to what your mind chatter says. The thing it's repeating most often, even if it sounds positive, indicates where you're stuck.

For instance, my client Janet talked nonstop about wanting to be thin. She was 5 feet 5 inches and weighed 250 pounds. She had been on every diet there was (and some there weren't) and she still hadn't lost weight permanently; the operational word is *permanently*. Two things were at work here. The first was the identifiable mind chatter: "I want to be thin." The second was the subconscious truth: "Thin is not for me." If, on a subconscious level, she had wanted to be thin, she would have been thin. Her mind was carrying out the good-little-girl syndrome, saying what it thought other people wanted to hear. Her body was acting out her reality. Her mind chatter was at war with her reality.

*When mind chatter talks nonstop about an area that doesn't change, you can be sure that's the area where your subconscious mind is holding you back.*

When mind chatter talks nonstop about an area that doesn't change, you can be sure that's the area where your subconscious mind is holding you back. You have two choices: You can either make peace with that area, or you can reprogram your subconscious. This book is about both reprogramming and making peace. You don't have to reprogram unless you really want to, and before you can reprogram, you have to make peace.

Is there an area in your life or your body that you constantly talk about

needing to change that doesn't change? _____

_____

_____

_____

_____

On Day 1 of the program, you will decide what your goal is for the next 21 days. What you have just written might be a good goal to work on.

## INTUITION: THE STILL, SMALL VOICE

You have another voice, a very little one, that's usually drowned out by mind chatter. It's called your intuition or your inner knowing, and it's always right. The reason you don't always listen to your intuition is that it usually takes the moral high ground, and usually wants you to do what you don't want to, or are afraid to do. It also tells you to do things without giving you a logical reason. Mind chatter often seems more logical.

I moved to California because my intuition told me I'd be happier there. It gave me no sound reasons for moving. My mind chatter told me all the reasons for staying in New York. It told me I didn't have a job out there, I couldn't make money, and I didn't have family there. My intuition just said move to California. I moved, and I am happy there. I have created a job, I make money, and my family visits me frequently. I've also created a family of friends who love and support me. The move to California introduced me to a group of inspirational teachers and leaders in metaphysics and personal growth, including Louise L. Hay. My studies in these areas led to the creation of *MetaFitness*, which Louise eventually published. As the concept of MetaFitness grew, the reason for the move to California became obvious: I would have taken a different road had I stayed in New York.

How often have you recognized before you did something that it wasn't going to work out? How often have you stayed stuck in a situation that wasn't working because your mind chatter told you staying was the right thing to do? Did you get sick? Did you get fired? Did you get divorced? Did you wish you'd left earlier? All my clients have said to me at one time or another, "If I'd only listened . . ."

Think about a time when your intuition told you something and you did not follow it.

What did it tell you? _____

_____

What did you do? _____

_____

What was the outcome? _____

_____

Can you remember what your mind chatter told you? _____

_____

Can you remember any body symptoms that you may not have associated with this situation at that time (illness, pain discomfort, weight gain or

loss)? _____

_____

_____

Can you see how intuition pointed to the thing you least wanted to do? Can you see how intuition pointed to what appeared to be the least safe thing you could do? Can you also see how intuition always points to the thing you ought to do?

Your intuition always recognizes the right choice. It is your guide. Some people believe it is God's way of communicating with us. Intuition often has no logic at all; it is just a quiet knowing. It just *is*. It is not attached to fear, but very often seems to stimulate fear because it points to the thing you least want to do. It often points to the hardest choice, although in the long run, it is the best choice. All too often we discount this voice until after a disaster has occurred.

The difference between mind chatter and intuition is that mind chatter usually speaks about fear or survival, powerlessness or negativity, and it always sounds very logical. Intuition often comes from left field and seems to be attached to nothing in particular. Mind chatter will keep you where you are. Intuition will move you forward.

# Establishing Your Baselines

♦

*The beginning is the most important part of the work.*

Plato
*The Republic*

♦

The human eye is deceptive. Very often it sees what it thinks it sees rather than what it actually sees. In 1981 I took a trip to Barbados with my mother and her friend Beanie. Recovering from my divorce, I had just gained 10 pounds and was feeling very fat. I weighed about 112 pounds. Although I wore a size 4, I kept talking about how fat I was. My mother got tired of listening to me and hauled out the measuring tape. She then proceeded to measure all three of us. As she took the measurements of my hips and thighs, and I saw the numbers, I realized I was very small. At the same time, I simply could not see myself as small in the mirror. My early programming mind chatter continued to tell me I was fat. What I needed was a baseline, a reality check. If you are 5 feet 4 inches tall, weigh 112 pounds, and wear size 4, you are thin. This optical illusion that is created by your own mind can work in reverse. I have had overweight clients who cannot see that they are overweight.

It is said that the mirror never lies. That's true—your eyes do. You cannot get an accurate picture from your mirror. Therefore, let's establish your baselines so that periodically you can give yourself a reality check. Knowing where you are starting from is the first step toward change.

## HOW DO YOU THINK OF YOUR BODY?

In Chapter 3 you were introduced to the concept of mirror work. In this section you will spend a little more time getting to know what you think about your body. Those thoughts may never change, but you will learn how to work with them so that they don't rule your life.

## EXERCISE

Stand or sit in front of a full-length mirror and look at your body. Write down everything you think about what you see.

## Example

I'm too fat.

I have cellulite on my hips, thighs, and buttocks.

I look awful from the rear.

I wish I had thinner knees.

I like my arches.

I have a great waist.

I have beautiful breasts.

My shoulders are lovely.

I like my ears but not my nose.

Your turn: _____

_____

_____

_____

_____

_____

_____

_____

_____

_____

_____

Do you like what you see? _____

Now it's time to get real. You need a measuring tape and access to a scale for this process. Undress. Using your measuring tape (cloth is best), measure your body as indicated on the chart that follows. You will repeat this again in 21 days; be sure you measure yourself in the same place each time. If you *must* wear clothes, be sure to wear the same ones each time you measure.

|  | *Baseline* | *21 Days* |
|---|---|---|
| Neck | _____ | _____ |
| Right upper arm | _____ | _____ |
| Right lower arm | _____ | _____ |
| Right wrist | _____ | _____ |

|                  | *Baseline* | *21 Days* |
|------------------|-----------|-----------|
| Left upper arm   | _____ | _____ |
| Left lower arm   | _____ | _____ |
| Left wrist       | _____ | _____ |
| Chest            | _____ | _____ |
| Breasts          | _____ | _____ |
| Midriff          | _____ | _____ |
| Waist            | _____ | _____ |
| Upper hips       | _____ | _____ |
| Middle hips      | _____ | _____ |
| Buttocks         | _____ | _____ |
| Right upper thigh | _____ | _____ |
| Right lower thigh | _____ | _____ |
| Right knee       | _____ | _____ |
| Right calf       | _____ | _____ |
| Right ankle      | _____ | _____ |
| Left upper thigh | _____ | _____ |
| Left lower thigh | _____ | _____ |
| Left knee        | _____ | _____ |
| Left calf        | _____ | _____ |
| Left ankle       | _____ | _____ |
| Weight           | _____ | _____ |
| Clothing size    |           |           |
|   Upper | _____ | _____ |
|   Lower | _____ | _____ |

*You are not your size or your weight.*

Wasn't that fun?

Watch for the trap. The trap is to judge the size and then go out and eat. It's not important to judge the size or weight. The size and weight aren't good or bad, they just *are*. And when you're ready, they will change (or not). You are not your size or your weight.

## WHY DO YOU EAT?

*Most people eat for every reason under the sun except hunger.*

As we noted in Chapter 1, most people eat for every reason under the sun except hunger. Ever notice that when you're upset, you eat? How about when you're angry? Ever spend an evening at home alone watching TV and find yourself spending half the time in your refrigerator?

The mind can hold only one thought at a time. If your attention is focused on food, it cannot be focused on feelings. Eating disorders are a perfect example of this process. Many people eat to avoid feeling painful or scary emotions. Others eat to make these painful or scary emotions manifest in physical discomfort.

These emotions include fear, terror, anger, rage, loss, hurt, powerlessness, self-denial, self-loathing. Can you think of times recently when you felt these emotions and reacted by eating? _____

_____

_____

_____

_____

_____

Take a look at your history. Remember and write down situations where these emotions resulted in eating. _____

_____

_____

_____

_____

_____

You may not be able to remember any incidents at this time. But now that you're alert to the possibility that this may be why you eat, you can come back to this exercise and fill it in later.

## Example

Tina came to me two years ago, upset about the fact that she was gaining weight uncontrollably. She had gained 13 pounds in six weeks and was afraid she couldn't stop. I asked her what was going on in her life. She replied that everything in her life was changing. She had moved out of her parents' home and was staying with friends until she decided where she wanted to live. She was between jobs, and she had just broken up with her boyfriend. I asked her what the *feeling* was. She started to cry and said, "I feel scared." I asked her if eating made her feel better and she said, "It always has, ever since I was a kid. Whenever I'm scared or lonely, I eat. I guess it started with my Nana, who always fed me when I was hurt or upset. Scrape your knee, get a cookie. One and one is two."

Your turn: _____

_____

_____

_____

_____

## LOOKING AT YOUR HISTORY OF WEIGHT GAIN AND LOSS

Let's look at your history of gain and loss. As closely as you remember, fill in the blanks, and stay out of the refrigerator.

| Year | Diet | Amount lost | Amount regained |
|------|------|-------------|-----------------|
| _____ | _____ | _____ | _____ |
| _____ | _____ | _____ | _____ |
| _____ | _____ | _____ | _____ |
| _____ | _____ | _____ | _____ |
| _____ | _____ | _____ | _____ |
| *Grand total* | _____ | _____ | _____ |

What did you discover? _____

_____

_____

## LOOKING AT YOUR HISTORY OF EXERCISE

How many times have you started to exercise "on a regular basis," only to stop days or weeks into the program? According to the May 1989 issue of *Club Business International*, 85 percent of all people who sign up for exercise programs drop out *before the first class*, and only 3 percent stay with a regular exercise program. Most people put everything but their bodies first. Exercise is for your body.

The problem with exercise is that in the past it has been linked with pain. "Go for the burn" and "No pain, no gain" were synonymous with the statement "Exercise is good for you." Another major problem with exercise programs is that many people who run them look down on people who are out of shape. Being out of shape is uncomfortable enough. You don't need to be made to feel worse.

*Most people put everything but their bodies first. Exercise is for your body.*

*The fact that you are not doing something simply because you don't want to is a very powerful statement.*

There are good reasons for people not to stick with exercise programs—which brings me to "reasons." Reasons, justifications, and excuses are synonymous terms, and they don't mean anything except that you have a reason, justification, or excuse for *not* doing something you don't want to do. The real reason you may not be exercising is that *you don't want to.* Now, isn't that refreshing?

Conversely, using "reasons" like "Exercise makes you healthy," "It keeps you fit," "It's good for your cardiovascular system" didn't convince you to exercise in the past. What makes you think it will convince you to exercise now? The only real reason to do anything is that you want to.

I have given myself all the right reasons to exercise. None of them ever made any difference. Only when I decided I wanted to exercise did I do it. And I had to make that decision on a daily basis. I now have a sign over my door that says "Because I want to," and I check in with that sign every day.

The fact that you are not doing something simply because you don't want to is a very powerful statement. You are in charge. The flip side of that coin is that you can exercise *because you want to.* You don't need any other reason.

Let's take a look at your history with exercise.

| Year | Program | Amount of time | When dropped |
|------|---------|----------------|--------------|
| ___ | ___ | ___ | ___ |
| ___ | ___ | ___ | ___ |
| ___ | ___ | ___ | ___ |
| ___ | ___ | ___ | ___ |
| ___ | ___ | ___ | ___ |

What did you discover about your exercise patterns from the past?

_____

_____

_____

_____

_____

If you are in a program and it works for you, this process does not apply to you. You may want to ask how much you like your program, and how you feel afterward. _____

_____

_____

Would you quit if you thought you "could get away with it"?

_____

Do you feel there's something missing that you would like to add to your program? _____

_____

_____

Do you keep adding to your program, making it more difficult and spending more and more time on exercise? _____

_____

Are you happy with your program and don't want any changes?

_____

What did you discover about yourself in relation to exercise?

_____

_____

_____

_____

_____

You have now established your baselines for your body and for your thinking about diet and exercise. Some of the things you wrote may surprise you. Clients have discovered things like they need a divorce, they want a lover, they want to move, they want to change careers—a whole bevy of things that at first glance don't appear to be connected to the size of their waist. Don't be surprised at what comes up for you. Pay attention to the things that come up strongly, no matter how preposterous they may seem. At the end of the book it will be fun to look back and see how your body, your attitudes, and your life have changed.

# The 21-Day Program

**H**abits can be changed in 21 days. This program is designed to help you change the habit of negative thinking that has prevented you from having the body you want.

In working with clients, I have discovered that most of them deal with not having the body they want by pretending the body they do have doesn't exist. This doesn't mean they don't tell themselves how fat or out of shape they are. Several times a day, every time they're confronted with a reflection or an ache, they dust their body off, yell at it, and then put it away until the next time. They don't work with their body on a consistent basis. These people expect their body to change just because they yell at it. That formula for change doesn't work.

The 21-Day Program accomplishes two things: awareness and change. It is designed to help you develop a positive relationship with your body, to help you bring your body out of the closet, spend time with it, and change it if you want to. In the 21-Day Program you will find numerous exercises structured to keep you physically aware all day. These exercises have very little to do with diet and exercise. You know all about diet and exercise. These exercises are designed to get you to a point where you can live comfortably and successfully with your body. You *can* diet and exercise if you want to, and chances are, if you do, you'll succeed. You'll succeed because you will come from a different place in yourself, a place of self-love and acceptance rather than self-loathing and hateful criticism.

The 21-Day Program will start you doing daily mind-body work. It will help you bring the processes of daily awareness exercises and creating affirmations into your life. It's a simple, full-body exercise plan, encompassing several different techniques and combining them with loving affirmations (to drown out your resistant, mind-chattering voice), that will give you the opportunity to actually enjoy physical exercise.

Through the physical awareness exercises you will learn which foods your body likes, and which foods are toxic to it. The 21-Day Program will teach you how to recognize your own nutritional needs and create a diet for yourself that is both pleasurable and effective.

The program introduces the concept of goal-setting as applied to the body. Through the goal-setting process you will be able to see what you've been asking of yourself, assess whether that's really what you want, and create realistic benchmarks for measuring success. Through the goal-setting process you will be able to create balance and harmony in your body. This balance and harmony will spill over into the rest of your life.

The 21-Day Program instills the habits of creating and having what you want in life because you are consciously and constantly working toward your goals. The repetition of the daily exercises puts down new grooves in your record of consciousness which will become your new life program.

Most important, the 21-Day Program works to build self-esteem and create self-love. It is only through self-acceptance that positive change can occur.

Finally, the 21-Day Program rewards you into making long-lasting change, instead of punishing you into making immediate but short-term changes.

The program has two benefits: (1) It's limited to 21 days; you have to commit only three weeks of your life to it. (2) If you do it, it changes everything.

The only way this program works is if you do it. It will not work if you just read it. You must commit yourself to the process.

## MAKING AN APPOINTMENT WITH YOURSELF

As I said earlier, I noticed recently that I am very careful to keep appointments that I have set up with other people, but I'm not careful to keep informal appointments that I set up with myself. I have come to realize that I put myself last. So I've developed a trick. I treat my body as if it were another person. I make appointments with it, and I honor them. For the purposes of this book, you are going to do unto yourself as you would do unto others. Make appointments with yourself and keep them. Remember, where "yourself" is concerned, it's easier not to keep your appointments than it is to keep them.

I have set a space toward the end of each day's exercises so that you can schedule an appointment with yourself for the following day. Occasionally, if I know that a process will be lengthy I have noted it so that you can schedule more time on the following day.

*It is only through self-acceptance that positive change can occur.*

When would you like to begin Day 1? You will need about 10 minutes.

APPOINTMENT WITH _____
(your name)

Day _____

Time _____

Have fun.

## GOAL-SETTING

In the beginning of my acquaintance with goal-setting, I thought that making a list at the start of the day, and getting through it, was setting goals. I had no long-range goals for my body, my career, or my life—and they all showed it. My life had a life of its own, my career went up and down, and so did my weight. Not only did they go up and down, but the only way I seemed to be able to keep them in any kind of order was by rigid control through pain, abuse, or drugs.

Instead of focusing my life in the direction I wanted it to go, I was trying to control it by focusing on all the things I didn't want to happen. I didn't want hardship, I didn't want failure, I didn't want to gain weight—and I got them all. Remember, there is no picture for *don't* or *won't* in the subconscious mind.

Through my work in business seminars and with Kathy Elster in New York, I have learned how to structure my life by setting positive goals for change so that I can work toward what I want instead of avoiding what I don't want.

### How to Set Goals

For the purposes of this book, I am going to give you a goal. You are also going to create a personal one for yourself. By the end of this program, as a result of working with these goals, you will learn to set your own goals for life. You will also learn how to work through the changes in your life so that you can have whatever you want with your body and your life without sacrifice, pain, or struggle.

GOAL:   I want to see positive results from completing every chapter and every exercise in this book.

Notice how you feel. Do you feel any kind of reaction or resistance to setting this goal? If you do, that's not unusual. This is a big goal, which will bring about change in your life. There's a part of you, as there is in all of us, that fears change because change is unfamiliar. The subconscious will hold on with all its might to what's familiar, even though what's familiar doesn't always work. When you experience resistance, notice it and continue with the program anyway.

Goals break down into simple tasks. Tasks, in general, are the small actions you need to perform each day to make the bigger goal happen.

Before going on, take the time to create a personal goal that's just for you. Make a list of what you want to accomplish in the next three weeks. The list can be as long or as short as you want. If it's very short and you accomplish it easily, it may show you how you underestimate your abilities and slow your forward motion. If it's very long, and you can't accomplish it, it may show you how you sabotage yourself by making unreasonable demands on yourself.

## Example

I want to get 10 pounds lighter.

I want to fit into my slim pants comfortably again.

I want to stop eating foods that aren't good for me.

I want to be on a regular exercise regimen again.

I want to like my body.

Your turn: _____

_____

_____

_____

_____

Now take a look at your list and choose one goal, the one that is the most important to you right now. It's okay if you wrote only one; that's the one that is most important to you at this time. If you want to, you can come back and add more, or change the one you initially chose. Your choice isn't set in cement. This is an exercise in becoming aware.

Now choose.

## Example

I want to like my body.

Your turn: _____

That is your personal goal at this time.

At the beginning of each day's exercises you are asked to refocus on your original goal. In the space provided at the top of the opening page for each day, restate your commitment to completing your goal by copying the goal as written above. Achieving your goal will mean doing the daily tasks and exercises for that day. Change occurs one day at a time.

In the space provided below, restate your personal goal one more time.

_____

Okay, now let's begin the process.

## Journal Work: An Introduction to Communicating with the Body

The mind and the body communicate with each other all the time. (They have to, because the brain regulates all body processes and functions which allow survival on a cellular level. This brain-to-cell communication happens faster than conscious thought, which is why you don't always understand what's going on with your body.) In order to be privy to this communication, you have to slow it down. To do this, you need to make your thoughts physical—by writing.

In the space provided, answer the following question. Write the first thought that comes into your head, regardless of whether it makes sense, is well written, is logical, embarrasses you, or seems ridiculous. Do not judge it.

"What does my body want?"

### Example

My body wants never to feel stuffed at the end of a meal again.

My body wants never to feel that I have to compulsively finish everything on my plate.

My body wants to feel energetic.

My body wants to dance.

My body wants to make love.

My body wants to wake and get up happy.

My body wants to look good in or out of clothes.

My body wants to be pain free.

My body wants to feel well.

My body wants to laugh.

My body wants to feel attractive.

My body wants to feel confident.

My body wants to feel relaxed.

My body wants to feel loved.

I want to love my body.

Your turn: _____

_____

_____

_____

_____

_____

_____

_____

_____

_____

Again, if you can think of only one thing, that's fine. You're not looking at an ideal, you're establishing a baseline. This is where you are at the moment.

Now that you have identified what your body wants, make a list of how you actually treat it, what you give it.

## Example

I usually finish everything on my plate (I'm always stuffed when I finish a meal).

I often go to bed late and feel tired in the morning.

I sometimes eat foods I know are toxic (sugar, wine, fatty foods), which rob my body of its natural energy.

I dance when I hear music that makes me feel good.

I take wonderful baths.

I slather my body with creams and lotions.

I'm exercising more regularly.

I also laugh a lot.

Your turn: _____

_____

_____

_____

_____

_____

_____

_____

_____

Did you notice that finding negative things was easier than finding positive things? That's okay. We have more practice in thinking negatively. Turning around takes time.

Think about your life and write down what you have always enjoyed in terms of exercise, sports, or movement. Some of you may have to go back to high school or earlier to find what you like or what you used to like.

## Example

I love to ski, swim, dance, ride horseback, hike, play tennis, row boats, canoe, fly kites, wrestle, mountain climb, rock climb. (You can even put in things you think you would like even if you've not yet tried them.)

Your turn: _____

_____

_____

_____

_____

Next, write down what you give your body in the way of exercise, sports, or movement at the present time.

## Example

I dance, and hike, and sometimes give myself the other things I like.

Your turn: _____

_____

_____

_____

_____

If you aren't doing anything at the moment, that's fine. You will when you want to.

If you could add one exercise that you like to your life in the next 21 days, what would it be? _____

_____

By when will you allow yourself to add it? _____

This is the end of Day 1, except for the final process, which you will do at the end of each day.

Reread what you have written and notice what you want, what you give yourself, and what you have learned about what you want to give yourself. What you want to give yourself is what this book is about.

It's almost the last exercise of the day, but before you go any further, it's time to make an appointment with yourself to work on your 21-Day Program tomorrow. Allow for up to 30 minutes.

*Make your appointment with yourself for tomorrow:*

Name: _____

Date: _____

Time: _____

## Evening Process: Ten End-of-the-Day Acknowledgments

In her book *Negaholics*, Cherie Carter-Scott teaches a process of ending the day by focusing on positive thought. Most of us end the day by reviewing what hasn't worked. "I didn't meet my deadline." "I didn't exercise." "I ate too much at dinner." "I drank too much." "I was rude." "I should have said . . ." "If only . . ." Focus instead on all the things that worked for you today.

### Example

1. Although I was tired, I got up on time.
2. I made the bed.
3. I met my deadline.
4. I spent quality time with my child today.
5. I ate well.
6. I finished four sections on my book.
7. I went to the movies.
8. I didn't buy the slacks-and-sweater outfit I don't need.
9. I learned something new about myself today.
10. I took a long walk when I got cranky, made myself feel better, and didn't yell at my sister.

Your turn (be sure to write 10). Remember, there's nothing too big or too small to be added to this list. Getting up may have been a feat today.

1. _____
2. _____
3. _____
4. _____

5. _____

6. _____

7. _____

8. _____

9. _____

10. _____

Sleep well, thinking about all the things that went right today.

## TASK-SETTING

Restate the goal as set for you on Day 1:

"I want to see positive results from completing every chapter and every exercise in this book."

Restate *your* personal goal from Day 1: _____

_____

Sometimes we fail to achieve our goals because they seem too big. But as noted above, "A journey of a thousand miles must begin with a single step." Tasks are the steps to achieving your goals. They are the manageable bits and pieces that achievement is made up of. Without tasks, you cannot achieve goals. Without goals, you cannot achieve success.

Over the next 20 days you will perform 20 simple tasks, one for each remaining day of the program, which will lead you to your goal. It may seem like a lot of work, but it has a purpose. In the remaining 20 days you will change a lot of habits, habits that were cemented however-many years ago. These habits are linked to tightly held subconscious programming; breaking them will be a challenge. So for these 20 days, I ask you to fully commit to the exercises, both physical and mental, even if they seem like a lot to do.

Now that your goal has been defined, think about what tasks you need to perform to achieve it. As an example, I will begin the process of setting tasks for the goal I set for you. After getting the hang of the process, you will create tasks for your own goals according to your own needs. After you decide what the tasks are, write them at the top of your daily program pages in the space provided. Each day you will perform the tasks you have set out to do.

(You may find you have achieved your goal before the end of three weeks. If you do, create another one, and go for it.)

Because you will understand your needs better as you go along, task-setting will be broken up into six sections. You will set new tasks every three or four days. Begin each day by restating your goal in writing and by writing your tasks for that day. Continually make certain that your tasks support your goal. You will know if they support your goal because you should be seeing measurable results. If you're not, reevaluate your tasks to make certain they are reasonable and that they support your goal. If they are, and you are still not seeing results, take a look at your goal and ask yourself whether it's what you, yourself, really want to achieve, or whether it's only what you think you ought to achieve, or whether you want to achieve it because it's someone else's goal. If it's not working for you, change to one that will.

### Example

GOAL:   I want to see positive results from completing every chapter and every exercise in this book.

## TODAY'S TASKS:

Set tasks for the next three days.

Complete all exercises for today.

Check off tasks completed.

## DAY 3:

(Re)read Chapter 1.

Complete all exercises.

Check off tasks completed.

Carry forward any uncompleted tasks.

## DAY 4:

(Re)read Chapter 2.

Complete all exercises.

Spend time writing in journal.

Check off tasks completed.

Carry forward any uncompleted tasks.

## DAY 5:

(Re)read Chapter 3.

Complete all exercises.

Write tasks for Days 6–9.

Check off tasks completed.

Carry forward any uncompleted tasks.

Your turn:

Personal goal: _____

_____

Today's tasks: _____

_____

_____

Day 3: _____

_____

_____

Day 4: _____

_____

_____

Day 5: _____

_____

_____

Congratulations! You have finished structuring your first tasks toward reaching your goal. Acknowledge yourself and move on. If that was hard for you, or if you couldn't do it, it's okay. Try to do it on a daily basis for a while. You may not be used to structuring your time in advance. It may take practice. Just don't get frustrated and give up.

You may also be experiencing considerable resistance to doing this. It may manifest as a physical discomfort. It may feel like tension, anger, confusion, frustration, or even illness. When I feel this kind of resistance, I recognize that I am about to make a major change in my life and my subconscious, which has a great deal invested in things remaining the same, is frightened. "Better a known evil than an unknown good."

## Journal Work: Negative Beliefs and Turnarounds

As I stated in Chapter 1, negative beliefs about ourselves permeate our existence. The thoughts are mean and constant and we don't always notice them consciously. To find out exactly what those negative thoughts are, so that you can turn them around, you need to write them down.

Answer the following question in the space provided. Write the first thought that comes into your head, regardless of whether it makes sense, is well written, is logical, is "good enough," embarrasses you, or seems ridiculous (do not judge your response).

"The worst things I think about myself are . . ."

**Example**

I'm too fat.

I don't know enough.

I'm not good enough.

I spend too much money thoughtlessly.

I'll never be any good.

I'm always late.

I don't take care of myself enough.

I'm not worthy of a relationship.

I'm stupid.

I don't exercise enough.

I'm not enough.

Your turn: _____

_____

_____

_____

_____

_____

_____

_____

_____

_____

_____

Looks pretty dismal, doesn't it? Making that list might also have been the easiest thing you have done all day. It's amazing how easy the negatives are. Most of us walk around thinking horrible things about ourselves all the time, wondering "How could anybody possibly like someone with all these faults?" or "When will they find out about the real me?"

The fact of the matter is, nothing that you have written above is true. Those "beliefs" are merely thoughts, air, nothing. As I said in Chapter 1, you made them up, or chose to believe what someone else made up, when you were just a child. And since you only made them up, you can make up different beliefs now. *You can change your mind.*

To change the way you think about yourself, you have to reframe (turn around) all those negative beliefs. You have to take the negative and make it positive. This may seem a bit absurd, and may feel strange at first, but you will discover that it works. I have always found this process fun. Your beliefs really will change. Remember, since thought is creative, thought comes first, and then you get to make yourself right.

The bottom line is, as your beliefs change, so will your life, your body, and the way you feel.

In the following exercise you will turn the negative beliefs on your list into positive statements. To accomplish this, you must make the negative appear to be the thing you most want in the world. You will use superlatives like *perfect*, *best*, and *greatest* to describe things you really hate about yourself. Don't be surprised if you have a hard time believing it in the beginning. Repetition will subdue the mental argument.

In the list that follows, my first negative belief is "I'm too fat." Now look at the first turnaround, "I'm the perfect weight for me at this time." Notice I didn't say "I'm the perfect weight." That would have been too hard to accept. My mind would have screamed, "What do you mean, *perfect?*" I would have spent so much time arguing that I would never have moved on to item number two. So I qualified the statement. I said "I am the perfect weight *for me* (not Christie Brinkley or Cher) at this time." Adding "for me" allows me to stop being mad at myself for not being someone else's perfect weight. I may never get to be someone else's perfect weight, but at least I can stop berating myself at this moment. Adding "at this time" implies that I might get to be another "perfect weight" later. With these two little additions I cut the mental argument off at the pass. I set up a statement I can believe.

Think of the turnarounds as a starting point. That makes the process easier; it also makes it believable. The following examples are ways of turning negative beliefs into positive statements. Any time you catch yourself making a negative statement, consciously substitute the positive. Another way to work with turnarounds is to write them 10 times every morning.

The reason for doing turnarounds is to change your mind. Your thoughts create your reality. As you change your thoughts, your reality changes. It's not the other way around.

| NEGATIVE BELIEF | TURNAROUND |
| --- | --- |
| I'm too fat. | I'm the perfect weight for me at this time. |
| I don't know enough. | I know all that I need to know right now. |
| I'm not good enough. | I'm perfect just as I am. |
| I spend too much money thoughtlessly. | I spend my money wisely and consciously. |
| I'll never be any good. | I'm getting better all the time. |
| I'm always late. | I always arrive at the right time. |
| I don't take care of myself enough. | I take perfect care of myself. |
| I'm not worthy of a relationship. | I am worthy of the right relationship for me. |

| | |
|---|---|
| I'm stupid. | I'm as smart as I need to be. |
| I don't exercise enough. | I spend the right amount of time exercising. |
| I'm not enough. | I am enough. |

Your turn:

| Negative Belief | Turnaround |
|---|---|
| _____ | _____ |
| _____ | _____ |
| _____ | _____ |
| _____ | _____ |
| _____ | _____ |
| _____ | _____ |
| _____ | _____ |
| _____ | _____ |
| _____ | _____ |

## Positive Beliefs

Now take a moment and dare to think of only wonderful things about yourself. Make a list of all those wonderful things. Write down even the things you're afraid to write down. "What will people think?" has no place here. No one is going to tell you that you're conceited, selfish, self-serving, self-absorbed, only interested in yourself, prideful, tooting your own horn, vain, or wrong. This program is about what _you_ think; it's also about what you haven't permitted yourself to think. _I_ know you're right about all those wonderful things—it's time you knew it too.

### Example

I'm beautiful.

I'm brilliant.

I'm fun.

I'm a good dancer.

I'm a good writer.

I'm an excellent teacher.

I'm a good entertainer.

I'm very disciplined about my work.

I have excellent taste.

I'm a good friend.

I'm sexy.

I'm a good lover.

I'm feminine.

I've got a good sense of humor.

I like people and people like me.

I'm a good mother, daughter, and sister.

I'm a good partner (business and personal).

I'm neat in both senses of the word.

Basically, I'm a fabulous person.

Your turn: (Take any one of mine you want; I'm also good at sharing.)

_____

_____

_____

_____

_____

_____

_____

_____

_____

_____

You can come back and add to this list any time you want. The ultimate goal is to come up with as many good qualities about yourself as you can—and believe them. If this isn't comfortable yet, that's okay. This is Day 2. Be patient with yourself. This material isn't easy.

*Make your appointment with yourself for tomorrow:*

Name: _____

Date: _____

Time: _____

Tomorrow is a long process. Be sure to allow sufficient time to finish comfortably.

## EVENING PROCESS

Look at, and remind yourself of, your goal.

Review today's tasks.

Check off those you have accomplished.

Carry over to tomorrow any you didn't finish today. (Know that it's okay if you haven't finished everything. You aren't in the "clean-plate club" any more.)

Notice what you didn't finish.

### Ten End-of-the-Day Acknowledgments

Remember, it's what you *did* that counts, not what you didn't do. Write 10 positive things you did today. Just as a reminder: A positive thing could even be staying in bed all day and resting; reading a trashy novel; watering the plants; or completing a 10-page report.

1. _____

2. _____

3. _____

4. _____

5. _____

6. _____

7. _____

8. _____

9. _____

10. _____

Good night. Sleep well, thinking about how wonderful you are and all those things that went right today.

## MIRROR WORK

Review your goals and tasks. Restate the goal as set for you on Day 1:

"I want to see positive results from completing every chapter and every exercise in this book."

### TODAY'S TASKS:

(Re)read Chapter 1.

Complete all exercises for today.

Check off tasks completed.

Carry forward any uncompleted tasks.

Do something nice for myself.

Restate *your* personal goal from Day 1: _____

_____

Today's tasks: _____

_____

_____

_____

_____

In Chapter 4, you had a chance to see how you look at yourself. Now you have the opportunity to turn all those negative pictures around.

Stand in front of the mirror with no clothes on. If that's not possible at this time, wear something in which you can see the outline of your body. If even that's not possible, wear what you usually wear and do the best you can. The idea is not to be mean to yourself.

Read aloud the positive statements listed below to each one of your body parts one part at a time. Allow your mind to hit you with its usual "Yeah, buts. . .". "Yeah, buts . . ." are what you have thought was true until now, and that's okay. They're going to change, but not before you become aware of what you've been thinking. Write down the negative statement. Repeat the next positive statement out loud, and again write down the mind's response. Continue in this manner until your mind is quiet. Go on to the next body part.

You will notice that the mind gets more vicious with some body parts than with others, and in some cases your mind even agrees with the positive statement. Eventually they all balance out, become positive, and even you begin to see how perfect your body really is.

So that you do not become overwhelmed, you will do only 12 body parts a day. After you have completed your entire face and body, you can repeat the process as often as you like until the end of the 21 days. You will find what happens to the way you see yourself very interesting. But unlike reading the last page of a novel before you've finished, you can't skip ahead. No matter how you try, you won't get an idea of what it is, or how it feels, until you actually have done the work.

## Example

Look at your face.

Say out loud, "My face is beautiful."

Write your response. "Sure, except for the lines around your mouth."

Repeat, "My face is beautiful."

Write your response. "Are you kidding? You have bags under your eyes, lines across your forehead, and a zit on your chin."

Repeat, "My face is beautiful."

Write your response. "It used to be beautiful when you weren't so fat."

Continue until you run out of responses. Remember, a sigh can be a response. If you need more space for responses, continue this exercise in your journal.

Your turn:

### EYES

| *Statement* | *Response* |
| --- | --- |
| "I have beautiful eyes." | _____ |
| "I have beautiful eyes." | _____ |
| "I have beautiful eyes." | _____ |
| "I have beautiful eyes." | _____ |
| "I have beautiful eyes." | _____ |

## NOSE

| *Statement* | *Response* |
| --- | --- |
| "I have the perfect nose." | _____ |
| "I have the perfect nose." | _____ |
| "I have the perfect nose." | _____ |
| "I have the perfect nose." | _____ |
| "I have the perfect nose." | _____ |

## MOUTH

| *Statement* | *Response* |
| --- | --- |
| "I have a lovely mouth." | _____ |
| "I have a lovely mouth." | _____ |
| "I have a lovely mouth." | _____ |
| "I have a lovely mouth." | _____ |
| "I have a lovely mouth." | _____ |

## CHEEKS

| *Statement* | *Response* |
| --- | --- |
| "I have great cheeks." | _____ |
| "I have great cheeks." | _____ |
| "I have great cheeks." | _____ |
| "I have great cheeks." | _____ |
| "I have great cheeks." | _____ |

## CHIN

| *Statement* | *Response* |
| --- | --- |
| "My chin is beautiful." | _____ |
| "My chin is beautiful." | _____ |
| "My chin is beautiful." | _____ |
| "My chin is beautiful." | _____ |
| "My chin is beautiful." | _____ |

3

## EARS

| *Statement* | *Response* |
| --- | --- |
| "My ears are perfect." | _____ |
| "My ears are perfect." | _____ |
| "My ears are perfect." | _____ |
| "My ears are perfect." | _____ |
| "My ears are perfect." | _____ |

## 3 FACE

| *Statement* | *Response* |
| --- | --- |
| "I have a beautiful face." | _____ |
| "I have a beautiful face." | _____ |
| "I have a beautiful face." | _____ |
| "I have a beautiful face." | _____ |
| "I have a beautiful face." | _____ |

## HAIR

| *Statement* | *Response* |
| --- | --- |
| "I have beautiful hair." | _____ |
| "I have beautiful hair." | _____ |
| "I have beautiful hair." | _____ |
| "I have beautiful hair." | _____ |
| "I have beautiful hair." | _____ |

## NECK

| *Statement* | *Response* |
| --- | --- |
| "My neck is perfect." | _____ |
| "My neck is perfect." | _____ |
| "My neck is perfect." | _____ |
| "My neck is perfect." | _____ |
| "My neck is perfect." | _____ |

## SHOULDERS

| *Statement* | *Response* |
| --- | --- |
| "I have beautiful/strong shoulders." | _____ |
| "I have beautiful/strong shoulders." | _____ |

"I have beautiful/strong shoulders."  _____

"I have beautiful/strong shoulders."  _____

"I have beautiful/strong shoulders."  _____

## UPPER ARMS

*Statement*                                          *Response*

"My upper arms are beautiful,
strong, and well defined."  _____

"My upper arms are beautiful,
strong, and well defined."  _____

"My upper arms are beautiful,
strong, and well defined."  _____

"My upper arms are beautiful,
strong, and well defined."  _____

"My upper arms are beautiful,
strong, and well defined."  _____

## ELBOWS

*Statement*                                          *Response*

"I have great elbows."  _____

"I have great elbows."  _____

"I have great elbows."  _____

"I have great elbows."  _____

"I have great elbows."  _____

## LOWER ARMS

*Statement*                                          *Response*

"My lower arms are strong and
beautiful."  _____

"My lower arms are strong and
beautiful."  _____

"My lower arms are strong and
beautiful."  _____

"My lower arms are strong and
beautiful."  _____

"My lower arms are strong and
beautiful."  _____

## WRISTS

| *Statement* | *Response* |
|---|---|
| "I have perfect wrists." | _____ |
| "I have perfect wrists." | _____ |
| "I have perfect wrists." | _____ |
| "I have perfect wrists." | _____ |
| "I have perfect wrists." | _____ |

## 3 ▶ HANDS

| *Statement* | *Response* |
|---|---|
| "My hands are beautiful, shapely, and strong." | _____ |
| "My hands are beautiful, shapely, and strong." | _____ |
| "My hands are beautiful, shapely, and strong." | _____ |
| "My hands are beautiful, shapely, and strong." | _____ |
| "My hands are beautiful, shapely, and strong." | _____ |

## FINGERS

| *Statement* | *Response* |
|---|---|
| "My fingers are perfect, shapely, strong, and beautiful." | _____ |
| "My fingers are perfect, shapely, strong, and beautiful." | _____ |
| "My fingers are perfect, shapely, strong, and beautiful." | _____ |
| "My fingers are perfect, shapely, strong, and beautiful." | _____ |
| "My fingers are perfect, shapely, strong, and beautiful." | _____ |

You have finished half your mirror exercise and you probably have some idea now of how nasty your thoughts about yourself can be. It's important that you don't argue with yourself. The vicious little voice that tells you all your faults will only yell louder if you argue. If you ignore it and keep telling yourself how beautiful and fabulous you are, it will eventually give up and agree with you. It takes time to change your mind. This is the first step.

On the other hand, you may not know that your mind is telling you anything awful. A client of mine once said, "My mind doesn't tell me awful things, it only tells me the truth." I asked her what the truth was. She said, "Oh, if I'm tired, it tells me I look tired, and if I have a zit on my chin it's sure to point it out. But these are true! Why shouldn't it tell me?" I asked her, "Does it tell you you are beautiful?" Her reply answered her question. "Of course not. Why should it tell me I'm beautiful?" Her mind was very quick to tell her all her faults, which she believed. It failed to tell her her virtues, which she considered vanity.

Your conscious mind sees and your subconscious mind interprets what you see according to the way it has been programmed. You have to reprogram your subconscious mind in order to allow your conscious mind to see your beauty. The tool for reprogramming is the affirmation.

## Create an Affirmation for the Day

Take a moment to review the thoughts that came into your head during the preceding process.

**Example**
My responses to the statement "My face is beautiful" were:

"Sure, except for the lines around my mouth."

"Are you kidding? You have bags under your eyes, lines across your forehead, and a zit on your chin."

"It used to be beautiful when you weren't so fat."

Choose the body part that you had a particularly negative reaction to and write down your responses again. _____

_____

_____

_____

_____

_____

Now look at those negative statements. What are they saying? How can you turn them around and make them positive? In looking at my statements, I see that aging, weight, and feeling "disfigured" are my sore points. I want to change these feelings by creating an affirmation. I have to memorize this affirmation because I must be able to repeat it, so I don't want to write a dissertation. One simple sentence will do.

Look at what you want the most. For me, it's to become more beautiful. Create a statement that confirms that you are becoming or getting what you want. If your mind sets up an argument, limit the statement a little. Notice I don't say "I *am* beautiful," but rather "I am becoming more beautiful every day." My mind would argue too vehemently with "I am beautiful," and the benefit of the affirmation would be lost. Your mind won't let you lie with affirmations, so you must move slowly.

**Example**

*Affirmation:* I am becoming more beautiful every day in every way.

Your turn: _____

_____

Copy this affirmation onto a separate piece of paper and place it in a spot where you will see it often during the day. Repeat it often.

*Make an appointment with yourself for tomorrow:*

Name: _____

Date: _____

Time: _____

Tomorrow is another long day. Be sure to allow yourself plenty of time to finish your processes.

## EVENING PROCESS

Look at, and remind yourself of, your goal.

Review today's tasks.

Check off those you have accomplished.

Carry over to tomorrow any unfinished tasks.

### Ten End-of-the-Day Acknowledgments

Write 10 positive things you did today. Remember, the littlest things count.

1. _____

2. _____

3. _____

4. _____

5. _____

6. _____

7. _____

8. _____

9. _____

10. _____

Good night. Sleep well. Dream about how special you are and how perfectly your day went.

*There is nothing either good nor bad but thinking makes it so.*

Shakespeare
*Hamlet*

## KEEPING TRACK OF WHAT YOU EAT AND HOW YOU FEEL

Review your goals and tasks. Restate the goal as set for you on Day 1:

"I want to see positive results from completing every chapter and every exercise in this book."

### TODAY'S TASKS:

(Re)read Chapter 2.

Complete all exercises for today.

Spend time writing in my journal.

Check off all tasks completed.

Carry forward any uncompleted tasks.

Restate *your* personal goal from Day 1: _____

_____

Today's tasks: _____

_____

_____

_____

_____

### Journal Work

To get the body they want, most people diet by eating the foods they are told to eat, in the amounts they are told to eat them. The 21-Day Program will teach you how to have the body you want by eating the foods your *body* likes to eat, in the amounts *it* likes to eat them. Before you can do that, you have to find out what those foods and amounts are. Right away you may have visions of hot fudge sundaes, pie à la mode, thick sauces, and calorie-laden dressings.

Not quite.

Not if you don't want to get sick or gain weight. Yes, you can eat what you want, but you have to learn to check in with your body. Your body will tell you; then it's up to you to listen . . . or not.

Write down every item you eat, along with estimated quantities, in a separate, small notebook—not your journal. (Your journal isn't portable enough, and it's something you will always want to keep. You may not always want to keep your food diary.) Then, after you've finished eating, write down how you feel. This is important. You will find that some days you feel fine after a candy bar and some days you feel awful. From this discovery (after the fact), you can begin to ask your body *before* you eat the candy bar whether or not it's a good idea. Some days it will be and some days it won't. Your body always knows and will tell you.

Also from this exercise you will begin to see which foods make your body feel healthy and which ones make it feel sluggish and uncomfortable. You will be able to determine which foods are best for you and create your own program for healthy, comfortable, fun eating.

Here's what your notebook can look like.

## DAY 1.

| Meal | What I ate | How I felt |
| --- | --- | --- |
| Breakfast | 1 cin/raisin muffin<br>1 tsp butter 1 tsp jam<br>coffee w/sweetener | Felt great all morning<br>Had lots of energy<br>Felt light |
| Lunch | 1 cup salad, let/tom/celery,<br>w/vinaigrette<br>vegetable soup, 1 rice cracker | Hi-energy afternoon<br>Felt light, very productive |
| Dinner | sautéed liver and onions,<br>broccoli, zucchini, and carrots<br>large hot fudge sundae | Ate everything on my plate<br>Felt stuffed<br>Felt woozy, slightly nauseated, like I had a ball in my stomach, couldn't lie down after dinner<br>Felt irritable and snappish |

You'll notice I began losing control during dinner when I ate everything on my plate even though I was full. To top it off with a hot fudge sundae was pure madness, but I did it anyway. It's as if, once headed down that path, there was no turning back. I used to do this a lot without realizing it. But now, because of my food diary, I do it less and less. I now know that my body does not like hot fudge sundaes, my mouth loves them. Whenever my mouth thinks it would like a hot fudge sundae, I ask myself whether I'm willing to feel that uncomfortable after eating. Most of the time I don't, once in a while I do, and I *always* feel uncomfortable.

My body knows what it likes and what it doesn't like. Sometimes I have a hard time understanding what it's saying, because my mouth is trained to like foods that don't always agree with my body, and sometimes my body likes foods my mouth hasn't acquired a taste for.

Once in a great while I get on a junk-food cycle. For whatever reason, usually when I'm on tour, I start eating junk. I usually start slowly. Some pretzels or cheese and crackers in the airport lounge, then perhaps a frozen yogurt start me off. The cycle escalates with french fries, hot dogs, and hot fudge sundaes, with my body pleading with me to stop. No matter how much I eat, it seems, I'm never satisfied. At times like these, I often find I'm hungrier at the end of a meal than when I started it. It took me some time to figure out what was going on. Now that I have, I rarely eat junk food, and never as a meal. Junk food has no nutrients. The body needs nutrients, not stuffing. Filling the body with empty calories just adds pounds, it does not get the motor going. Although I was eating a lot when I was stuffing myself with junk, I was starving my body.

Once I figured this out, I had to figure out how to stop the cycle. I learned to eat one *deliberately* good meal a day. Once the cycle was broken, my body stopped asking for excess food.

Please don't misunderstand me. Sometimes it's okay to eat a candy bar or other junk food. There's a big difference between being on a junk-food cycle or a candy binge and eating the occasional bit of junk. I have found that if I deny myself junk food altogether, the feelings of deprivation set up a craving. Once again, it's a balance between some and too much.

If you have never eaten "healthy" food, you won't know what it is. The way to introduce your body to healthy food is to introduce it to the list in Appendix B. Substitute foods on that list for foods you have been used to eating. The three things that have to leave your diet are fat, sugar, and overly processed foods. Limit your intake of fried, greasy foods, all deli, dairy products, most animal products, and processed, sugary desserts. That's a beginning.

Learn to be in tune with your body. It will tell you what to eat. You need to practice, first by noticing how you feel after you eat, then by paying attention to your body's signals before you eat. Keep asking your body, "Okay, body, what do you want?" Your body always knows. When I listen, I always feel good; when I don't listen, I don't. It never fails. Begin your food journal today. Start now.

| Meal/Time | What I ate | How I felt |
|---|---|---|
| Breakfast: _____ | | |
| _____ | | |
| _____ | | |
| Lunch: _____ | | |
| _____ | | |
| _____ | | |

(Snack): _____

_____

Dinner: _____

_____

_____

_____

(Snack): _____

_____

## Mirror Work Continued from Day 3

To change the subject completely, at some time today, it will be appropriate to finish the mirror work begun during Day 3. (See page 53.) It is important to finish this process, because it helps you establish the hot spots that you will want to work on during the remaining days of the program.

## UPPER BACK

*Statement*                                    *Response*

"I have a beautiful upper back; it
is strong and well defined."        _____

"I have a beautiful upper back; it
is strong and well defined."        _____

"I have a beautiful upper back; it
is strong and well defined."        _____

"I have a beautiful upper back; it
is strong and well defined."        _____

"I have a beautiful upper back; it
is strong and well defined."        _____

## MIDDLE BACK

*Statement*                                    *Response*

"My middle back is beautiful,
strong, and sturdy."                 _____

"My middle back is beautiful,
strong, and sturdy."                 _____

"My middle back is beautiful, strong, and sturdy." _____

"My middle back is beautiful, strong, and sturdy." _____

"My middle back is beautiful, strong, and sturdy." _____

## LOWER BACK

*Statement*                                    *Response*

"I have a perfect lower back; it is strong, sturdy, and beautiful." _____

"I have a perfect lower back; it is strong, sturdy, and beautiful." _____

"I have a perfect lower back; it is strong, sturdy, and beautiful." _____

"I have a perfect lower back; it is strong, sturdy, and beautiful." _____

"I have a perfect lower back; it is strong, sturdy, and beautiful." _____

## CHEST

*Statement*                                    *Response*

"I have a strong, beautiful, shapely chest." _____

"I have a strong, beautiful, shapely chest." _____

"I have a strong, beautiful, shapely chest." _____

"I have a strong, beautiful, shapely chest." _____

"I have a strong, beautiful, shapely chest." _____

## MIDRIFF

*Statement*                                    *Response*

"My midriff is toned and well defined." _____

"My midriff is toned and well defined." _____

"My midriff is toned and well defined." _____

"My midriff is toned and well defined." _____

"My midriff is toned and well defined." _____

## WAIST

| *Statement* | *Response* |
| --- | --- |
| "My waist is exactly right." | _____ |
| "My waist is exactly right." | _____ |
| "My waist is exactly right." | _____ |
| "My waist is exactly right." | _____ |
| "My waist is exactly right." | _____ |

## STOMACH

| *Statement* | *Response* |
| --- | --- |
| "My stomach is beautiful; it is strong, toned, and just right." | _____ |
| "My stomach is beautiful; it is strong, toned, and just right." | _____ |
| "My stomach is beautiful; it is strong, toned, and just right." | _____ |
| "My stomach is beautiful; it is strong, toned, and just right." | _____ |
| "My stomach is beautiful; it is strong, toned, and just right." | _____ |

## HIPS

| *Statement* | *Response* |
| --- | --- |
| "I have great hips." | _____ |
| "I have great hips." | _____ |
| "I have great hips." | _____ |
| "I have great hips." | _____ |
| "I have great hips." | _____ |

## BUTTOCKS

| Statement | Response |
|---|---|
| "I love my perfect buttocks." | _____ |
| "I love my perfect buttocks." | _____ |
| "I love my perfect buttocks." | _____ |
| "I love my perfect buttocks." | _____ |
| "I love my perfect buttocks." | _____ |

## THIGHS

| Statement | Response |
|---|---|
| "My thighs are great, strong, toned, and well defined." | _____ |
| "My thighs are great, strong, toned, and well defined." | _____ |
| "My thighs are great, strong, toned, and well defined." | _____ |
| "My thighs are great, strong, toned, and well defined." | _____ |
| "My thighs are great, strong, toned, and well defined." | _____ |

## KNEES

| Statement | Response |
|---|---|
| "I have shapely knees." | _____ |
| "I have shapely knees." | _____ |
| "I have shapely knees." | _____ |
| "I have shapely knees." | _____ |
| "I have shapely knees." | _____ |

## CALVES

| Statement | Response |
|---|---|
| "My calves are beautiful." | _____ |
| "My calves are beautiful." | _____ |
| "My calves are beautiful." | _____ |

4

"My calves are beautiful." _____

"My calves are beautiful." _____

## ANKLES

*Statement*                                          *Response*

"I have great ankles." _____

"I have great ankles." _____

"I have great ankles." _____

"I have great ankles." _____

"I have great ankles." _____

## FEET

*Statement*                                          *Response*

"I have neat feet." _____

"I have neat feet." _____

"I have neat feet." _____

"I have neat feet." _____

"I have neat feet." _____

## TOES

*Statement*                                          *Response*

"I have lovely toes." _____

"I have lovely toes." _____

"I have lovely toes." _____

"I have lovely toes." _____

"I have lovely toes." _____

## SKIN

*Statement*                                          *Response*

"My skin is beautiful." _____

"My skin is beautiful." _____

"My skin is beautiful." _____

"My skin is beautiful." _____

"My skin is beautiful." _____

## POSTURE

*Statement*                                              *Response*

"I have great posture."              _____

"I have great posture."              _____

"I have great posture."              _____

"I have great posture."              _____

"I have great posture."              _____

## BODY

*Statement*                                              *Response*

"I love my body. It is perfect just the way it is."

_____

"I love my body. It is perfect just the way it is."

_____

"I love my body. It is perfect just the way it is."

_____

"I love my body. It is perfect just the way it is."

_____

"I love my body. It is perfect just the way it is."

_____

### Affirmation Exercise

Review your negative thoughts from the mirror process. Choose a really awful one and turn it around to make it your positive affirmation for the day.

**Example**

*Statement*                          *Response*

"I have great hips."          Sure, for someone who has saddlebags.

*Affirmation:* My hips are perfect, shapely, toned, and well defined. I look terrific in jeans.

If you don't believe the affirmation, that's okay. Just don't go so far from what you believe that you spend the day angry with yourself. What I did here was to stretch the truth. My hips *are* shapely and well defined. There may be too much of them, but they are still shapely and well defined. Sometimes you can use words like *sturdy* or *strong*, which you might not particularly like but which are still positive, to change your mind about a body part you don't like. Sturdy and strong are a lot better than gross and disgusting. The point of the exercise is to find something positive to say about any part of yourself you don't like.

Your turn:

| *Statement* | *Response* |
|---|---|
|  |  |

Affirmation: _____

_____

Copy this affirmation onto a separate piece of paper and put it somewhere where you can look at it often. Say it to yourself as many times as possible during the day.

*Make an appointment with yourself for tomorrow:*

Name: _____

Date: _____

Book time: _____

Exercise time: _____

*Note:* Tomorrow you will begin the physical exercise program. Please be sure you have exercise clothes that are comfortable to work out in, music that makes you want to move, and one- or two-pound barbells and two- to five-pound ankle weights you will begin to use later on. Please set aside 30 minutes to an hour and a half to exercise and additional time to work in the book.

## EVENING PROCESS

Look at, and remind yourself of, your goal.

Review today's tasks.

Check off those you have accomplished.

Carry over to tomorrow anything you didn't finish; know that it's okay.

## Ten End-of-the-Day Acknowledgments

Write 10 positive things. Remember, the littlest things count, and it's what you did that matters, not what you didn't do.

1. _____

2. _____

3. _____

4. _____

5. _____

6. _____

7. _____

8. _____

9. _____

10. _____

Good night. Sleep well. Dream about how special you are and how perfectly your day went.

## EXERCISE PROGRAM AND AFFIRMATIONS

Review your goals and tasks. Restate the goal as set for you on Day 1:

> "I want to see positive results from completing every chapter and every exercise in this book."

### TODAY'S TASKS:

(Re)read Chapter 3.

Complete all exercises for today.

Write tasks for Days 6–9.

Check off tasks completed.

Carry forward any uncompleted tasks.

Restate *your* personal goal from Day 1: _____

_____

Today's tasks: _____

_____

_____

_____

*Write tasks for Days 6–9:*

Day 6: _____

_____

Day 7: _____

_____

Day 8: _____

_____

_____

Day 9: _____

_____

_____

## Exercise Program

It's time to begin your exercise program. You may love this part, you may not. What's important here is to notice how you feel while you exercise. Use your journal. When you're finished exercising, write down what your mind told you about the exercises and the way you felt during the process.

Comments might look like, "This exercise feels great." "I used to be able to do this movement easily." "I never could do this before." "I hate this exercise." "This would be easy if I weren't so fat."

If you can, exercise in front of a mirror. Watch yourself. Put on your favorite music; music that has a steady beat is preferable.

Begin with the 22 warmup exercises on pages 76–102. Each day you will add three exercises. By the end of the 21 days you will have a 60-to-90–minute conditioning plan structured for optimal results. This program will help you strengthen and tone your muscles and give your body definition. You should expect to have more energy when you finish each day's exercises than when you start. You should also expect to feel better. You may want to augment this program with low-impact or nonimpact aerobics, or bench-step aerobics. Remember, if it hurts, *stop.*

To increase the effectiveness of the exercises, you will work with resistance (weights). Starting with tomorrow's exercises, you will need a pair of one- or two-pound barbells.

## AffirMotions

The major difference between my exercise program and everyone else's is the affirmations I include with each exercise. I call this process AffirMotions: combining Affirmations with Motion. As hundreds of my students have discovered, to get more out of an exercise you must think positively while doing it.

Ever notice when you exercise, very often you tell yourself how awful you are or how bad you feel (your mind chatter at work)? You look in the mirror during class and see all the things you are doing wrong. And you tell yourself how uncoordinated you are, how inept you are compared to the person next to you, how awful you look today. Ever notice how, when an exercise is hard, you concentrate on the difficulty?

In order for your body to do a good job, it has to think it's doing a good job. If you tell your body how strong it is, what a good job it's doing, and how beautiful it is, that's what your body will think it's doing and *that's what you will experience.* For example, crunches (an abdominal exercise) used to be difficult for me. My stomach would begin to hurt quite soon after I began the exercise. When I started affirming how strong my stomach was, and what a good job I was doing, I noticed a total difference in feeling and ability. The affirmations I use are: "My stomach is strong," "I love to exercise my abdominals," and "My abdominal muscles are doing a wonderful job today." They work! Using these affirmations may seem silly to you at first—it often does to my students when they first begin—but after a while, it will become natural. You will notice a positive difference in the way you feel and the way you perform exercises. You will also see a positive difference in your body.

The reason these affirmations work is that every cell in your body holds memory. Every time you have a thought, either positive or negative, that thought is stored in every cell (just as it is stored in your subconscious). Every time you look at yourself, or think of your body, and then think a negative thought, it is stored. Every time you move, thoughts are communicated from the cells to your subconscious mind. Those thoughts determine how you feel, they affect your health, they affect how you look, and they affect the way you experience life.

It's time to reprogram those cells so that they are filled with positive thoughts. As you reprogram your body, you will become a walking positive affirmation. Every move you make will release positive thoughts into your subconscious. As you release positive thoughts throughout your body and your subconscious, you will look and feel better and better. You will feel more joyous being you and living in the body you live in.

Each exercise works a particular part of the body. Each part of the body has its own series of affirmations. Choose the ones you enjoy saying and begin to repeat them while you exercise. As I said, you may feel a bit silly doing this at first. Find a way that works for you. Many of my students whisper the affirmations to themselves; some say them to themselves in their mind. But they all notice a positive difference in the way they feel when they say the affirmations, and wouldn't stop saying them.

Begin your physical exercise program with the warmup, Exercises 1–22.

**5**

# 1 SALUTE (heart and lungs)

Stand with your feet hip width apart, knees (soft) slightly bent, arms resting at your sides. Tighten your buttocks and abdominals. Tuck your buttocks under in a slight C curve. Inhale deeply as you raise your arms outward and up to meet above your head. Exhale fully, as you lower your arms out and down to cross slightly in front of you. Repeat this exercise 4 times as you say affirmations.

## AFFIRMATIONS FOR HEART AND LUNGS

**Heart:** *My heart is strong and healthy. I am safe both giving and receiving love. I love myself and others. I am loved.*

**Lungs:** *My lungs are strong and healthy. I take in life fully and joyously. I love my life.*

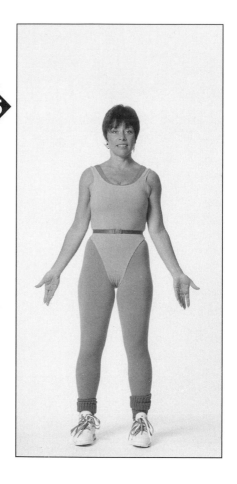

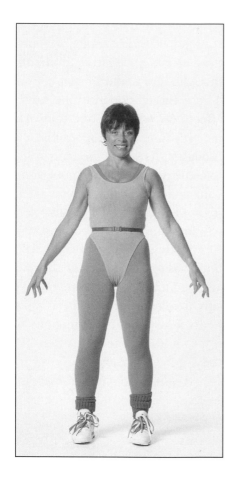

5

# 2 HEAD TURNS (neck)

Stand with your feet hip width apart, legs straight, knees soft (slightly bent). Tighten your buttocks and abdominals. Tuck your buttocks under in a slight C curve. Rest your arms by your sides. Relax your shoulders. Breathe normally. Keep your shoulders still and turn your head to the right; hold 2 seconds. Turn your head to the left; hold 2 seconds. Repeat 8 times in each direction, as you say your affirmations.

## AFFIRMATIONS FOR THE NECK

*My neck is strong and beautiful; it moves easily and without tension. I see all sides of every issue with ease. I see endless ways of accomplishing everything I need to do. I am safe and peaceful.*

5

# 3 HEAD ROLLS (neck)

Stand as in Exercise 2. Turn your head to the right. Now circle your head down and then up to the left, and then down and then up to the right. Repeat 8 times in each direction, as you say your affirmations for the neck, as in Exercise 2.

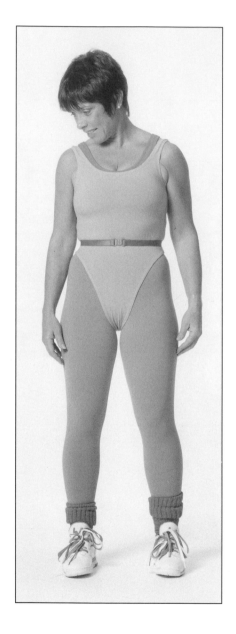 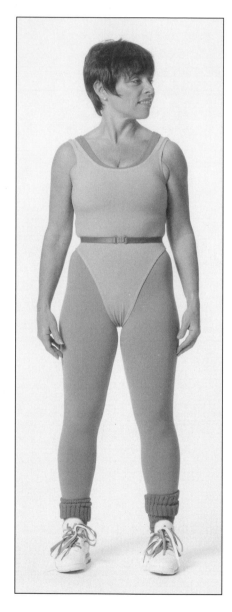

5

# 4 SHOULDER ROLLS (shoulders)

Stand with your feet hip width apart, knees soft. Relax your shoulders and rest your arms by your sides. Tighten your buttocks and abdominals. Tuck your buttocks under in a slight C curve. Breathe normally. Circle your shoulders forward, up, backward, and down. Repeat 4 times as you say the affirmations for the shoulders. Circle your shoulders backward, up, forward, and down. Repeat 4 times while saying your affirmations. Repeat both sequences twice.

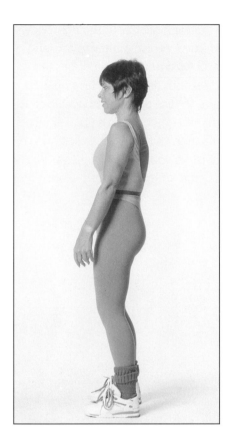

## AFFIRMATIONS FOR SHOULDERS

*My shoulders are strong and beautiful. They are proud and tension-free. My burdens are light; they support my growth. I choose to allow all my experiences to be joyous and loving.*

5

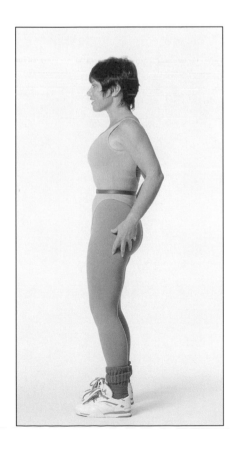

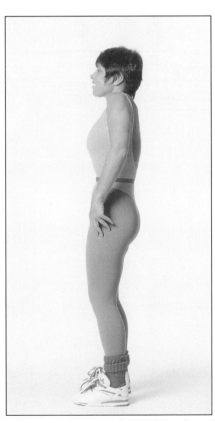

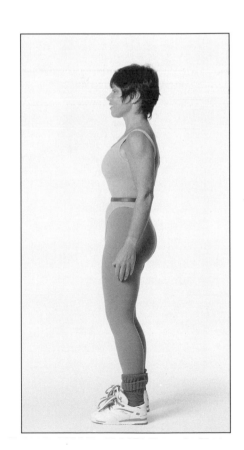

# 5 ARM TWISTS (arms)

Stand with your feet hip width apart, knees soft. Keep your shoulders relaxed and your arms slightly bent. Tighten your buttocks and abdominals. Tuck your buttocks under in a slight C curve. Raise both arms slightly bent and out to your sides. Your right arm should face up, your left arm should face down and back. Keep your hips still and lean your torso slightly to the right. Now shift your torso slightly to the left and twist both arms in opposite directions (left arm to face up, right arm to face down and back). Get a rhythm going and continue in this manner, shifting your torso and twisting your arms 16 times as you say the affirmations for the arms.

## AFFIRMATIONS FOR ARMS

*My arms are beautiful, toned, and well defined. They are strong and smooth. I embrace my life with joy. I am safe as I reach for my goals, my beautiful arms bringing me all that is good.*

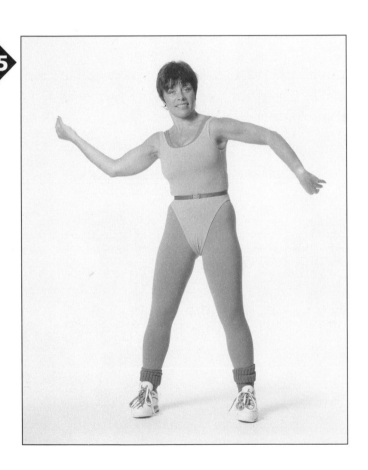

# 6 SWIM (shoulders and arms)

Stand with your feet slightly wider than hip width apart, legs straight and knees soft. Tighten your buttocks and abdominals. Tuck your buttocks under in a slight C curve. Lean your torso slightly forward and, using full arm rotation, circle your arms around, one at a time, as if you were swimming (doing the crawl). Do 16 forward, 16 over your right leg, 16 over your left leg, and 16 forward again as you repeat the affirmations for shoulders and arms.

---

### AFFIRMATIONS FOR SHOULDERS AND ARMS

**Shoulders:** *My shoulders are strong and beautiful. They are proud and tension-free. My burdens are light; they support my growth. I choose to allow all my experiences to be joyous and loving.*

**Arms:** *My arms are beautiful, toned, and well defined. They are strong and smooth. I embrace my life with joy. I am safe as I reach for my goals, my beautiful arms bringing me all that is good.*

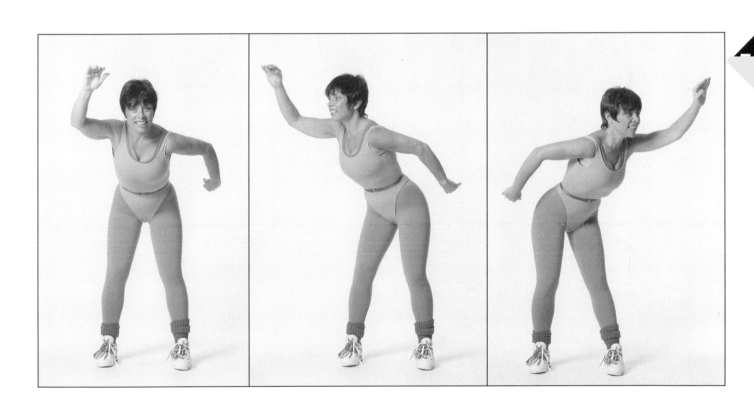

# 7 TORSO SHIFTS (midriff)

*Side to Side:* Stand with your feet hip width apart, knees soft. Tighten your buttocks and abdominals. Tuck your buttocks under in a slight C curve. Keeping shoulders relaxed, raise both arms outward to form a T. Keeping your hips still, shift your torso to the right. Now shift it to the left. Get a rhythm going and repeat 16 times as you say the affirmations for the midriff.

Now shift twice to the right, twice to the left. Again, get a rhythm going and do the double shifts 8 times as you say the affirmations.

**5**

*Back and Forth:* Now, holding your hips still, shift your torso forward, then back. Be sure to maintain control and repeat 16 times. Again say the affirmations for the midriff.

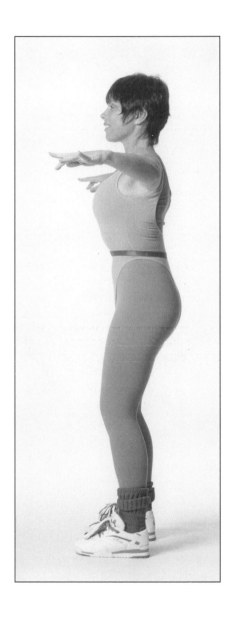

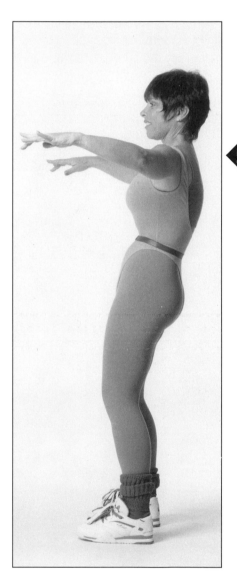

5

# 8 HIP WAGS (hips)

Stand with your feet hip width apart, knees soft. Tighten your buttocks and abdominals. Tuck your buttocks under in a slight C curve. Bend your right arm and raise your right hand up and away from your body as you thrust your left hip to the left. Now lower your right hand, raise your left, and thrust your right hip to the right. Wag your hips from side to side in this manner 16 times as you say the affirmations for the hips.

| AFFIRMATIONS FOR HIPS |
|:---:|
| *My hips are perfect, strong, toned, shapely, and flexible. I am free to move forward in my life in perfect balance, with joy and laughter. There are joy and balance in every day and everything I do.* |

# 9 KNEE WAGS (knees and ankles)

Stand with your feet together, knees three-quarters bent. Tighten your buttocks and abdominals. Tuck your buttocks under in a slight C curve. Keep your weight centered and your arms by your sides.

Bend your right arm, bringing your right hand up toward your shoulder and shift your knees to the right. Lower your right arm as you bend your left and shift your knees to the left. First you will lean on the outside of your right foot, the inside of your left foot. Then you will lean on the outside of your left foot, the inside of your right foot. Repeat knee wags 16 times in each direction as you say the affirmations for the knees and ankles.

---

### AFFIRMATIONS FOR KNEES AND ANKLES

**Knees:** *I love my knees. They are beautiful, shapely, strong, and flexible. My life is balanced. I work and play equally, with joy and delight. I bend and flow with ease.*

**Ankles:** *I have beautiful ankles. They are strong, toned, and flexible. I am safe. I move with ease and flexibility, and communicate freely. All is well with me in my world.*

**5**

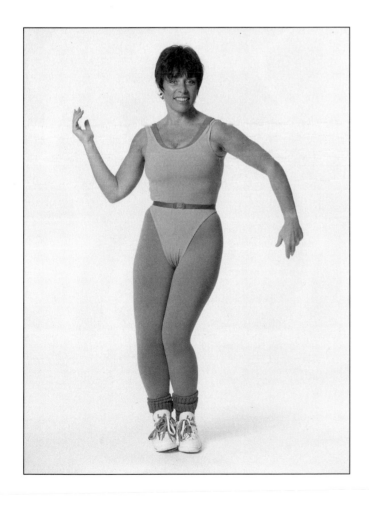

# 10 ANKLE CIRCLES (ankles)

Stand next to a wall or hold on to the back of a chair or sofa with one hand. Stand with your feet together, knees soft. Tighten your buttocks and abdominals. Tuck your buttocks under in a slight C curve. Rest your other arm at your side. Keep your legs straight, knees soft, and raise your left foot slightly off the floor in front of you. Flex your foot and circle it 4 times clockwise and 4 times counterclockwise. Repeat with your right foot. Repeat the sequence twice as you say the affirmations for the ankles.

> **AFFIRMATIONS FOR ANKLES**
>
> *I have beautiful ankles. They are strong, toned, and flexible. I am safe. I move with ease and flexibility, and communicate freely. All is well with me in my world.*

**5**

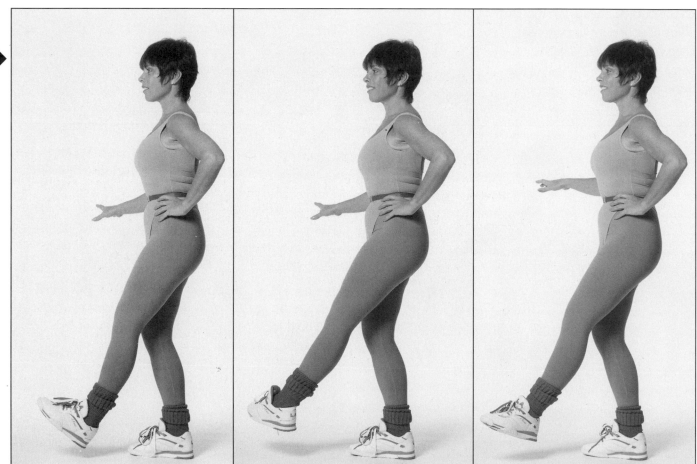

# 11 FOOT CURLS (feet)

Stand with your feet together, legs straight, knees soft. Rest your hands at your sides. Tighten your buttocks and abdominals. Tuck your buttocks under in a slight C curve. Curl your feet round so that you are leaning on the outsides of both feet. Hold 4 seconds and feel the stretch on the outsides of your feet. Now relax and flatten your feet again. Next, lift your toes up toward your face, stretching the soles and strengthening the insteps. Hold 4 seconds and release. Repeat curl-flatten-lift-flatten 8 times as you say the affirmations for the feet.

---

### AFFIRMATIONS FOR FEET

*I love my feet. They are beautiful, strong, and flexible. I love my life and the way I choose to live. My foundation is strong and secure. Because of my strong foundation, I am safe following my dreams. I love taking care of myself. All is well and perfect in my life.*

**5**

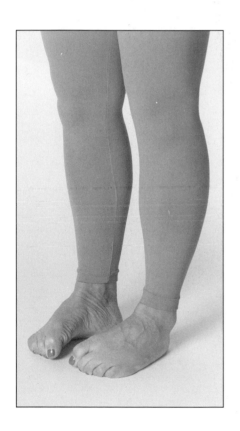 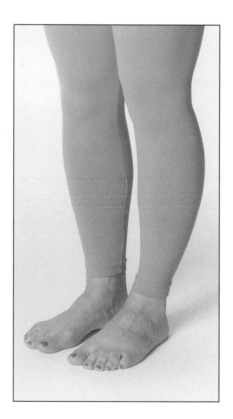 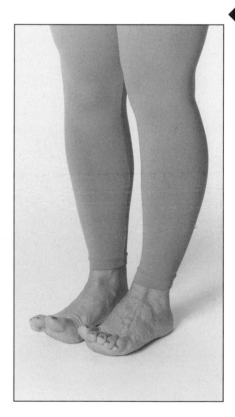

# 12 CROSS STEP (legs)

*Front:* Stand with your feet together, legs straight, knees soft. Tighten your buttocks and abdominals. Tuck your buttocks under in a slight C curve. Bend and raise your left arm while you cross your right foot in front of your left foot. Touch your toes to the floor in front and to the side of your left foot. Lower your arm and return your foot to its original spot. Bend and raise your right arm while you cross your left foot in front of your right foot, touching your toes to the floor. Lower your arm and return your foot to its original spot. Get a rhythm going and repeat 16 times as you say the affirmations for the legs.

5

*Back:* Raise your right arm and twist your body left as you cross your right leg behind you, touching your toes to the floor. Lower your arm and return your foot to its original spot. Raise your left arm and twist your body right as you cross your left leg behind you, touching your toes to the floor. Return your foot to its original spot and repeat 16 times. Perform the series twice as you say the affirmations for the legs.

### AFFIRMATIONS FOR LEGS

*My legs are beautiful, strong, shapely, flexible, toned, and well defined. They move with grace. I forgive all childhood trespasses, real and imagined, and go forward with positive feelings. I love life and enjoy all my experiences, past and present. I move forward in life with grace and ease. I am safe now and in the future.*

**5**

## 13 HEEL LIFTS (legs, [specifically hamstrings], mid-back, and shoulders)

Stand with feet slightly wider than hip width apart, knees soft, hands resting at your sides. Tighten your buttocks and abdominals. Tuck your buttocks under in a slight C curve. Breathe normally.

Keeping your feet apart, step with your right foot and raise both arms above your head and out to the sides. Now, keeping knees wide, kick your left foot up behind and pull your arms down.

Step left and raise arms, kick right and pull arms down. Get a rhythm going and repeat 16 sets (32 times) as you say the affirmations for the legs and flexibility.

## AFFIRMATIONS FOR LEGS AND FLEXIBILITY

*My legs are strong and beautiful. I move forward in my life with ease, releasing all anger from the past and welcoming my future with joy. I am safe and flexible in my life. All is well now and in the future.*

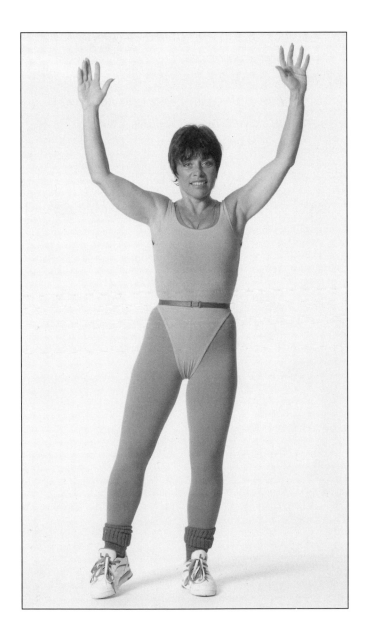

# 14 HEEL TAPS (legs, shoulders, and mid-back)

Stand with feet slightly wider than hip width apart, knees soft, hands resting at your sides. Tighten your buttocks and abdominals. Tuck your buttocks under in a slight C curve. Breathe normally.

Step with your right foot. Keeping arms wide, stretch them out in front of you. Bend your right knee as you bring your left foot out in front and thrust your buttocks out behind you. Tap your left heel to the floor as you pull your arms back.

Step with your left foot. Keeping your arms wide, stretch them out in front of you. Bend your left knee as you bring your right foot out in front and thrust your buttocks out behind you. Tap your right heel to the floor as you pull your arms back.

Repeat 16 sets (32 times) as you say the affirmations for legs, chest, and upper back.

## AFFIRMATIONS FOR LEGS, CHEST, AND UPPER BACK

**Legs:** *My legs are beautiful, strong, shapely, flexible, toned, and well defined. They move with grace. I forgive all childhood trespasses, real and imagined, and go forward with positive feelings. I love life and enjoy all my experiences, past and present. I move forward in life with grace and ease. I am safe now and in the future.*

**Chest:** *My chest is beautiful, well defined, strong, and powerful. I love my life. I am safe. I love being loved. I love giving and receiving. I take in and utilize all of life's loving experiences.*

**Upper back:** *My upper back is strong, straight, and beautiful. I carry joy; I move with ease. I love and approve of myself. Life supports and loves me. I am safe, loving and being loved.*

# 15 KNEE TO ELBOW STRETCH (arms, back, legs, abdominals, and midriff)

Stand with your feet slightly wider than hip width apart, knees soft, arms resting at your sides. Tighten your buttocks and abdominals. Breathe normally. Lean your weight on your right leg and bring your left knee up as you twist your torso slightly down and to the left. Bend your right arm and bring your right elbow down to touch your left knee.

Now straighten your left leg out, tapping your left toes on the floor as you straighten your torso and reach up and out with your right arm. Bring your left knee and right elbow to meet again and repeat entire movement 8 times as you say the affirmations.

Change sides. Step with, and place your weight on, your left leg as you bring your right knee up to meet your left elbow. Straighten your right leg out, tapping your right toes on the floor as you reach up and out with your left arm. Bring your knee and elbow in to meet again and repeat 8 times as you say the affirmations.

Repeat sequence twice.

## AFFIRMATIONS FOR ARMS, BACK, ABDOMINALS, LEGS, AND MIDRIFF

**Arms:** *I have beautiful arms. They are strong, toned, and well defined. I embrace my life with ease. All is well in my world.*

**Back:** *My back is beautiful, strong, sturdy, and well defined. I am supported by life. I am safe in all that I know. I am fully capable and supported.*

**Abdominals:** *I have a beautiful stomach. It is strong and well defined. I digest new ideas with ease and am safe following my intuition.*

**Legs:** *I have beautiful legs. They are strong and shapely. I move forward in my life with ease. I release all past hurts. I love my life.*

**Midriff:** *My midriff is beautiful and shapely. I am safe feeling all of my emotions. My emotions are life-supporting and I feel them with joy.*

5

# 16 BUTTERFLY SALUTE (arms, chest, upper back, and shoulders)

*Backward Circle:* Stand straight with feet slightly wider than hip width apart, arms resting at your sides. Tighten your buttocks and abdominals. Tuck your buttocks under in a slight C curve. Bring your left elbow up and back and place the back of your hand on your cheek. Now straighten your arm and circle it up behind you. Make a full circle back and down and bring it to rest at your side.

Repeat with your right arm. Alternating arms, repeat 8 sets (16 times) as you say the affirmations.

**5**

*Forward Circle:* Change directions with your arms. Standing as for the backward circle, circle your left arm back and around, bending your elbow and placing the back of your hand on your cheek. Straighten your arm in front of you and continue the circular motion until your arm rests at your side. Repeat with your right arm. Alternating arms, repeat 8 sets (16 times) while saying the affirmations.

---

### AFFIRMATIONS FOR ARMS, CHEST, UPPER BACK, AND SHOULDERS

**Arms:** *I love my arms. They are strong and beautiful. I embrace my life with joy and ease.*

**Shoulders:** *My shoulders are beautiful, strong, proud, and straight. I carry my life lightly. I take joy in all that I do.*

**Back:** *I have a great back. It is strong, beautiful, and well defined. I am safe in my life, fully supported, and capable of handling all of life's situations.*

**Chest:** *I love my chest. It is shapely, strong, beautiful, and well defined. I welcome love into my life. I am safe giving and receiving love. I nurture myself and others with joy and ease and feel fulfilled in all that I do.*

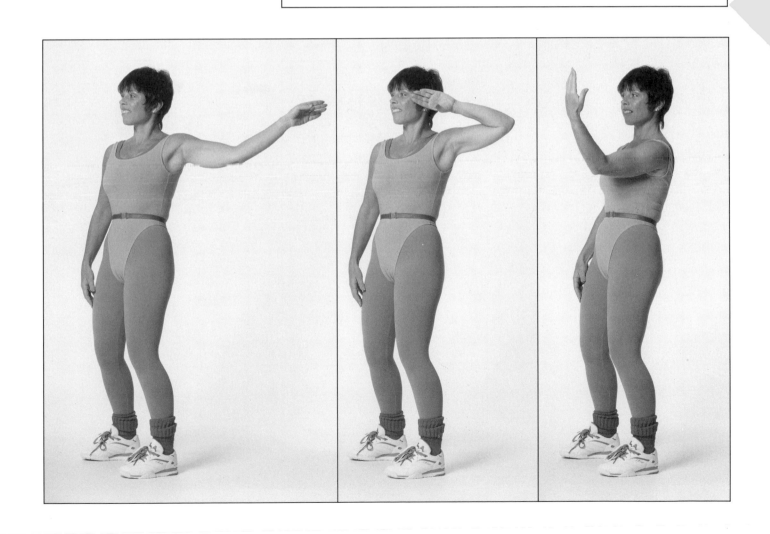

Stand with your feet slightly wider than hip width apart, knees soft, shoulders relaxed, hands placed on your hips. Tighten your buttocks and abdominals. Tuck your buttocks under in a slight C curve. Breathe normally.

Thrust your pelvis out (buttocks back), then tuck your pelvis under. Get a rhythm going and repeat 16 times as you repeat your affirmations.

**5**

## AFFIRMATIONS FOR ABDOMINALS, LOWER BACK, HIPS, AND PELVIS

**Abdominals:** *I love my stomach. It is strong and toned. I digest new ideas with ease and am safe following my intuition.*

**Lower back:** *My lower back is strong, shapely, and very beautiful. All my needs are met in the present time. I am safe and supported.*

**Hips:** *I have great hips. They are shapely, strong, and lovely to look at. I am balanced in my life, moving forward with ease.*

**Pelvis:** *I love my pelvis. It is beautiful and strong. I am creative and love my sexuality. My creativity flows with ease. It is safe for me to be sexual.*

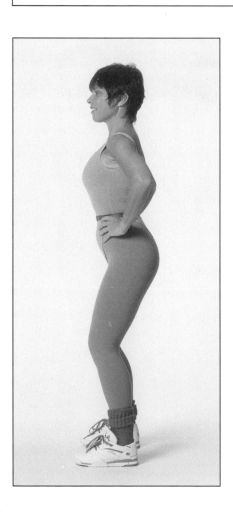 

# 18 SHOULDER STRETCH (shoulders and upper back)

Stand with your feet wide apart. Tighten your buttocks and abdominals and, keeping your back flat, lean forward, placing your hands on your knees.

Keeping your knees pressed back, slowly stretch your right shoulder toward your left knee. Hold 10 to 20 seconds.

Now stretch your left shoulder toward your right knee. Hold 10 to 20 seconds.

Repeat twice as you say your affirmations.

## AFFIRMATIONS FOR SHOULDERS AND UPPER BACK

**Shoulders:** *I love my shoulders. They are strong and very beautiful. I release my burdens and carry my responsibilities with ease.*

**Upper back:** *My back is beautiful, strong, and well defined. I am supported by life. I am safe, fully supported, and well taken care of.*

5

# 19 HIP FLEXOR STRETCH (flexibility—hip flexors or psoas)

Stand with feet wider than hip width apart, knees soft, arms raised at your sides. Tighten your buttocks and abdominals. Tuck your buttocks under in a slight C curve.

Lower your left arm and turn it to face palm up as you turn right. Your right foot should be flat on the floor, facing right. Your right arm should be straight out in front, shoulder height. Your left foot should face right with your heel lifted and your arm back, palm up.

Keeping your buttocks and abdominals tight and your buttocks tucked in a slight C curve, bend both knees as you lower your left knee toward the floor. (Be sure your right knee is directly over your right heel as you lower your left knee to the floor. If you notice your right knee thrusting further forward, place your feet wider apart.) Stand straight again. Repeat 8 times and then hold your left knee down for a count of 8 seconds. Repeat twice and change sides as you say the affirmations for flexibility and hips.

Do 2 sets facing left and lowering your right knee toward the floor. Be sure your left knee stays over your left heel as you lower your right knee to the floor.

5

**5**

Stand with your feet wide apart and turn to the right with both feet facing right. Lean forward slightly. Tighten your buttocks and abdominals and, keeping your left leg straight and your left heel close to the floor, step forward and bend your right knee as far as possible. Be sure your right knee stays over the right heel. (If your knee moves further forward than your heel, stretch your left foot further back.) Hold this position 10 to 20 seconds as you say the affirmations for flexibility and legs.

Repeat the same movement on your left side, your left knee bent over the left heel, your right leg stretched out behind you with the right heel as close to the floor as possible.

### AFFIRMATIONS FOR FLEXIBILITY AND LEGS

**Flexibility:** *I am flexible in all areas of my life.*
*It is easy for me to move in any and all directions.*
**Legs:** *I love my legs.*
*They are beautiful, strong, shapely, and lovely to look at.*
*They carry me with grace and ease.*
*I move forward in my life with joy and ease,*
*releasing my past hurts and frustrations and welcoming my future with delight.*

**5**

# 21  HAMSTRING STRETCH (flexibility—legs [hamstrings])

*Forward Lean:* Stand with your feet slightly wider than hip width apart. Relax your shoulders. Tighten your buttocks and abdominals, and tuck your buttocks under in a slight C curve. Turn right. Both feet should face right. Place your hands on your hips and, keeping your chest uplifted and your back straight, bend your right knee over your ankle as you lean your weight forward. Keep your left leg straight and your heel on the floor. Hold this stretching position 10 to 20 seconds while you say the affirmations for flexibility and legs in Exercise 20, then release. Change sides and repeat, stretching the right leg behind, 10 to 20 seconds while you say the affirmations.

*Backward Lean:* Standing as in the forward lean, place your weight on your left leg, bend your left knee, and lean back onto your left leg. Keep your right leg straight, flex your right foot, and bring the toes up toward your face. Place your hands on the thigh of your (bent) left leg for balance, thrust your buttocks out, and hold 10 to 20 seconds.

Stand straight and turn left. Repeat the exercise facing left. Bend your right knee, place your hands on your right thigh, and flex your left foot, bring the toes up toward your face. Hold 10 to 20 seconds as you say the affirmations for flexibility and legs in Exercise 20.

5

# 22 QUADRICEP STRETCH (flexibility—legs)

Stand with your feet together. Balance yourself as in photo or hold on to the back of a chair, couch, or the wall for balance. Tighten your buttocks and abdominals and tuck your buttocks under in a slight C curve. Lean your weight on your right leg and, keeping your knees parallel and close together, bend your left knee and raise your foot behind you. Grasp your left ankle or instep and hold 10 to 20 seconds as you say the affirmations for legs and flexibility in Exercise 20. Change sides and repeat with your right leg.

**5**

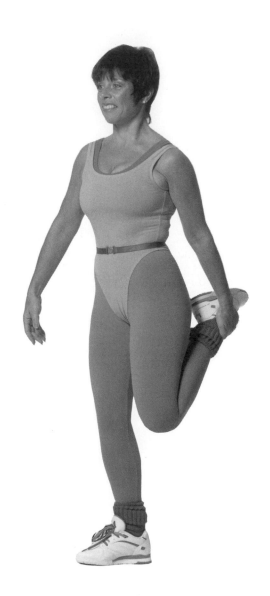

## Journal Work

Take out your journal and write down how you felt during the exercises. How do you feel right now? Which exercises did you like best? Do you have more or less energy now that you've finished the warmup? Are you tired? Hungry? Do you like the way you feel? Does your body like the way it feels? Is this something you want to do tomorrow? If not, what exercise would you prefer doing?

## Mind Chatter Turnarounds

In your journal, write down all the negative things your mind told you while you were exercising.

**Example**

> This is ridiculous.
>
> I feel like a cow.
>
> If you think I'm going to do this every day, you're out of your mind.
>
> Wow, my knees hurt!
>
> I'm so stiff.
>
> That hurts.

Your turn: _____

_____

_____

_____

_____

_____

_____

_____

> Now turn these negative statements around.

**Example**

> There is value in my doing these exercises.
>
> I am more and more graceful every day.

Doing these exercises is fun.

My knees feel better and stronger. They love to exercise.

My muscles are getting stronger and looser every day.

I do only exercises that feel good.

Your turn: _____

_____

_____

_____

_____

_____

_____

_____

_____

_____

When you first start creating turnarounds, you may question them. The object is to turn your negative thoughts into positive ones. To turn them around you have to start somewhere. Your mind will follow, but you have to lead it.

## Becoming Aware Exercise

Continue to notice how you feel after you eat. Make sure you make the appropriate entries in your food diary each time you eat. "Don't put off writing for later what you feel right now" is the motto to go by at this time. If you wait, you may not remember. It is important for you to notice how you feel. Remember, you won't usually feel anything right away. It takes from 30 minutes to 2 hours for food to affect your body (unless it's really toxic—then it takes just minutes).

## Affirmation Exercise

Create an affirmation for today. How do you want to feel? How do you want to look? Make a list of the ways you want to feel, what you want, and the way you want to look.

### Example

I want to feel energized.

I want to look thin.

I want to finish all my work.

I want to feel loved.

I want to look beautiful.

I want to have time to play.

Your turn: _____

_____

_____

_____

_____

Look over your list and create your affirmation.

**Examples**

I feel loved. I finish all my work and have plenty of time to play.

I am looking more beautiful every day.

Your turn: _____

_____

_____

Copy this affirmation onto a separate piece of paper and tack it up somewhere where you will see it often during the day.

*Make your appointment with yourself for tomorrow:*

Name: _____

Date: _____

Book time: _____

Exercise time: _____

## EVENING PROCESS

Look at, and remind yourself of, your goal.

Review today's tasks.

Check off those you have accomplished.

Carry over to tomorrow any you didn't finish today.

## Ten End-of-the-Day Acknowledgments

1. _____
2. _____
3. _____
4. _____
5. _____
6. _____
7. _____
8. _____
9. _____
10. _____

5

DAY 6

## VISUALIZATIONS

Review your goals and tasks. Restate the goal as set for you on Day 1:

"I want to see positive results from completing every chapter and every exercise in this book."

Restate *your* personal goal from Day 1: _____

_____

Review today's tasks, which you wrote yesterday. _____

_____

_____

_____

_____

A visualization is a mental picture, image, or feeling. Visualizing is a way of clarifying the picture of what you want so that when you ask for it, your mind knows exactly what you're asking for. Visualizations help your mind create what you want.

Very often we say we want to be rich, but we have no idea of what rich looks like. If you say you want to be rich and all you picture is not being poor, you are not giving your mind clear instructions. The mind responds to clear instructions both verbally and visually. If you want to be rich, the mind will meet your picture of what rich means to you. You have to be specific, and know that things happen in their own time. If you want to be thin and the picture you have of yourself is heavy, you may lose weight but gain it back, or you may never lose weight, or you may lose the weight and never see that you have lost it. First, you need to change the picture of your body in your mind, and the rest will follow.

Visualization is the clarifying picture that goes with the words. Just as the subconscious mind cannot tell the difference between something you say you want and something you say you "don't" want, it cannot tell the difference between a picture of something you want and a picture of something you don't want. It's a good idea to visualize the things you *want* rather than things you *don't* want.

When you consciously create visualizations and use them with affirmations, you enhance the power of the affirmation to create what you want. Since you are creating the body and the life that you want, you can make up any picture you choose. Combine this picture with your affirmation and move toward your goal. Take the affirmations from Day 5 and create your visualizations.

## Examples

I feel loved. I finish all my work and have plenty of time to play.

*Sample visualization:* I see someone who loves me smiling at me while I put the finishing touches on a piece of work. When I finish, I take that person's hand and we go out for a walk in the park.

I am looking more beautiful every day.

*Sample visualization:* I see myself in a mirror in my mind. I am looking more and more beautiful. I smile at myself in the mirror and see how beautiful I am (I don't see someone else's beautiful face, I see my face beautiful).

The next time I say my affirmations I will combine them with the visualizations I have just created.

Your turn: Restate your affirmation and create a visualization for it.

_____

_____

_____

_____

_____

_____

_____

Use your journal if you need more room, or if you wish to create more than one visualization or have made more than one affirmation.

The next time you say your affirmations, combine them with the visualization. Remember, it is your thoughts and the pictures in your mind that create your reality. They create where you live, how much money you have, your job, and even your relationships. They also create your body. When you change your thoughts about your body, you'll change your body.

# DAILY EXERCISES

## Becoming Aware Exercise

Continue to notice how you feel after you eat and write the observations in your food diary.

## Physical Exercises

Before beginning each day's new exercises, be sure you have completed the warmup starting on page 76 in Day 5. This is an add-on program. You begin with Day 5, do the warmup, and then add on each day's exercises. It will take 21 days to put the entire program together. From then on, you will have a complete, all-around exercise routine that is structured to help you stay fit and healthy. If you incorporate this program into your daily life, you can create the body you want without effort or struggle.

## A Word About Weights

You are not doing strength training. You are doing resistance training. The purpose is not to weigh yourself down and work yourself until you reach muscle exhaustion or lactic acid buildup, but simply to work against the light weights to give your muscles more toning.

Keep it light, keep it simple, keep it fun.

When using weights, always keep your knees soft, always exhale on the "exertion" (the difficult part), and always inhale on the "return" (the easy part). Know that most injuries occur on the return, so, although it is easier than the exertion, you must pay attention and maintain careful control.

Add the following exercises to the warmup from Day 5.

**6**

# 23 BARBELL PRESSES (chest or pectorals)

Lie on your back, knees bent, feet flat on the floor. Hold a 1- or 2-pound barbell in each hand by your shoulders. The ends of the barbells should be facing each other.

Keeping your arms shoulder distance apart, exhale and slowly raise your hands straight up away from your body. Inhale and slowly lower your hands toward your shoulders.

Repeat 12 times and rest 30 seconds. Do 2 sets of 12 repetitions, resting 30 seconds between sets, as you repeat the affirmations for the chest.

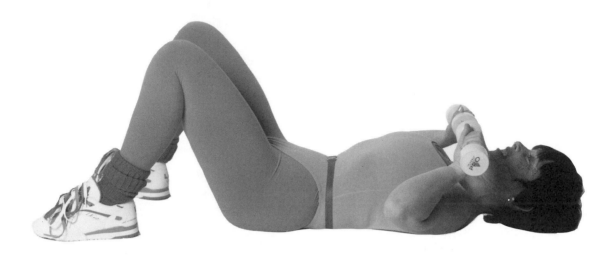

# 24 FLIES (chest or pectorals)

Lie on your back, knees bent, feet flat on the floor. With a 1- or 2-pound barbell in each hand, bring your arms up in front of you, wrists straight and facing each other, arms slightly bent. Inhale and slowly lower your bent arms out to the side.

Exhale and bring your arms up; your hands should meet over your chest. Keep the motion smooth and controlled and repeat 12 times. Rest 30 seconds and repeat again as you say the affirmations for the chest.

### AFFIRMATIONS FOR THE CHEST

*I love my chest. It is strong and beautiful. I am safe giving and receiving love. I give and receive love with ease and joy. Love delights me.*

6

# 25 REVERSE FLIES (back)

Stand with your left foot forward and your right foot back. Lean slightly forward and place your left hand and left knee on a table, stool, or the back of a chair for support. Place both barbells in your right hand. Keep your buttocks and abdominals tight, your buttocks tucked in a slight C curve, and your knees soft. Exhale and raise your bent right arm out to the side at an angle slightly lower than shoulder height. Inhale and lower it in front of you again. Repeat 12 times and change sides. Repeat 12 times with your left arm. Do the series twice as you say the affirmations for your back.

6

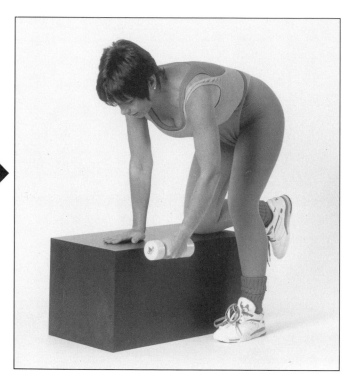

## Mind Chatter Turnarounds

In your journal, write down all the negative things your mind told you while you were exercising and turn them around.

## Affirmation Exercise

Create an affirmation for today as described on pages 70–71. Write it down in your journal and be sure to look at it periodically during the day.

*Make an appointment with yourself for tomorrow:*

Name: _____

Date: _____

Book time: _____

Exercise time: _____

## EVENING PROCESS

Look at your goal.

Review today's tasks.

Check off those you have accomplished.

Carry over to tomorrow anything you didn't finish today.

### Ten End-of-the-Day Acknowledgments

1. _____
2. _____
3. _____
4. _____
5. _____
6. _____
7. _____
8. _____
9. _____
10. _____

## "NURTURES" AND "CHEAP THRILLS"

Restate the goal as set for you on Day 1 and your personal goal.

_____

_____

_____

_____

Review and restate today's tasks: _____

_____

_____

_____

_____

Most of us are so busy doing nice things for other people, we forget to do nice things for ourselves. The self likes to be rewarded. Rewards make it feel good. There is no rule (although most of us seem to feel there is) that says you have to wait for someone else to reward you. You can reward yourself.

Cherie Carter-Scott uses the term *nurtures* to mean nice things you consciously do for yourself—things that make you feel good. The operational word is *consciously*. You may do lots of nice things for yourself, but if you don't notice them or take them for granted, they aren't nurturing. Nice things can range from a walk on the beach to the purchase of a new car (provided you can afford the new car).

Make a list of all the things you like to do for yourself.

**Example**

Get a manicure, pedicure.

Have my hair done.

114

Buy flowers.

Watch a sunset.

Hike a mountain.

Walk in the rain.

Buy a new outfit.

Go out for dinner.

Get a massage.

Take a scented bath (with candles, incense, and soft music).

Sleep late.

Read in bed.

Notice I didn't say anything like "hot fudge sundae" or "an expensive new dress." A hot fudge sundae, which is toxic to me, or an expensive new dress, which is beyond my present budget, would not be nurtures. They would be considered "cheap thrills." Cheap thrills are the things you pretend are a good idea to do when you really know they aren't. The rationales you use could be, "I've been good all week." "I haven't spent any money lately." "I've exercised extra hard." You may actually say to yourself, "I deserve it." We've all done this. We do something we pretend is good for us and then spend the rest of the day, or longer, mentally and/or physically beating ourselves up about it. The point is, when you're going to do something for yourself, *be conscious*. First be conscious that you're doing it, and then be certain that it's a nurture and not a cheap thrill.

Make your nurtures list: _____

_____

_____

_____

_____

_____

_____

_____

_____

_____

Now that you have a good list of nurtures, choose one, write it down, and give it to yourself some time today. You will do this every day.

Today's nurture: _____

**7**

### Becoming Aware Exercise

Continue to notice how you feel after you eat and write your observations in your food diary.

### Physical Exercises

Continue the exercise program from Days 5 and 6 and add the following exercises.

# 26 BICEP CURL (arms)

Stand with your feet hip width apart. Tighten your buttocks and abdominals, and tuck your buttocks under in a slight C curve. With a 1- or 2-pound barbell in each hand, bend your arms slightly and keep your elbows close to your waist.

Exhale, and, keeping your arms close to your sides, raise your right barbell up toward your shoulder. Keeping your wrist straight, and your arm controlled, inhale and slowly lower the barbell. Repeat with the left hand. Do 12 repetitions with each

hand and rest 30 seconds. Repeat the series twice, always resting 30 seconds between sets. Be sure to say your affirmations while you perform the bicep curl.

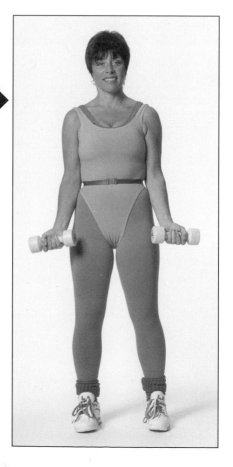
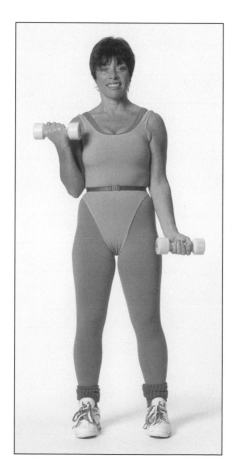
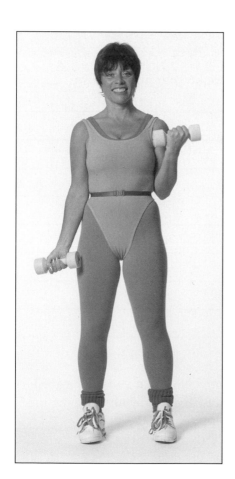

7

# 27 CROSS CURL (arms)

Stand as in Exercise 26. Place both barbells in your right hand and place your right hand on your hip. Keeping your left arm bent slightly, cross it in front of you to form a 90-degree angle with your body. Exhale and raise the barbells to your left shoulder (be sure your wrist is straight). Inhale and, using control, lower the barbells to the starting position. Repeat 12 times and change hands. Repeat 12 times with your right hand. Repeat the series twice as you say the affirmations for arms.

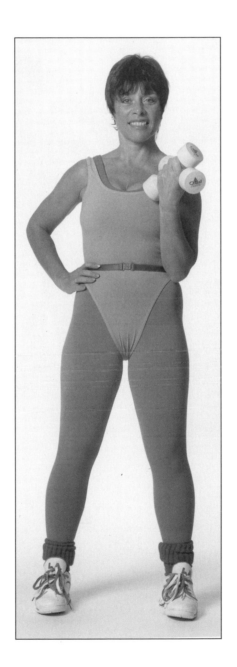

7

# 28 CURL OUT (arms)

Stand as in Exercise 26. Hold barbells in your left hand with your palm up. Keep your elbow close to your side, and your arm turned out away from center. Your arm should form a 90-degree angle away from your body. Exhale and raise your left hand to your shoulder. Inhale and lower it to the original position. Repeat with your right hand. Always be sure the return is controlled. Repeat 12 times with each hand. Do the series twice as you say the affirmations for arms.

## Mind Chatter Turnarounds

In your journal, write down all the negative things your mind told you while you were exercising and turn them around.

## Affirmation Exercise

Create an affirmation for today, following the instructions on pages 70–71. Write it down in your journal and be sure to refer to it during the day.

## Visualization Exercise

Take a moment to look at, hear, and feel your affirmation. Now create a visualization for that affirmation, following the instructions of Day 6, on pages 107–108, and write it in your journal.

## Week in Review

Take 10 minutes to look over your journal and review what you've learned about yourself in relationship to your body. What did you learn about the way you talk to yourself? How are you feeling after you eat? Have you noticed which foods make you feel good and which make you feel uncomfortable? Are you more comfortable with your affirmations? How does it feel to be more aware of your likes and dislikes? How does it feel to exercise? Where do you need to spend more time? What haven't you done? What are you consistently not doing? Remember, it's *your* program. For it to work, you have to work it. Have fun and continue on.

*Make an appointment with yourself for tomorrow:*

Name: _____

Date: _____

Book time: _____

Exercise time: _____

## EVENING PROCESS

Review your goal.

Review today's tasks.

Check off those you have accomplished.

Carry over to tomorrow anything you didn't finish today.

## Ten End-of-the-Day Acknowledgments

1. _____
2. _____
3. _____
4. _____
5. _____
6. _____
7. _____
8. _____
9. _____
10. _____

## YOUR BODY AS A MESSAGE MACHINE

Restate the goal as set for you on Day 1 and your personal goal.

_____

_____

_____

_____

Review and restate today's tasks: _____

_____

_____

_____

_____

As I stated in Chapter 2, your body is a message machine. It tells you not only what is going on in your body, but what is going on in your life. Each part of the body represents some aspect of your life. Through its tensions, its little aches and pains, your body lets you know what's happening. Unfortunately, we often treat our bodies like the messengers were treated in early Greek times. If the emperor didn't like the news, he killed the messenger. If we don't like our bodies' news, we punish it. "Go for the burn" has never been a friendly statement. Fatness, soreness, sickness, and fatigue are body messages. They're not things to get mad at, they're things to listen to and to address.

If you're overweight, out of shape, frequently ill, often tired, and physically sore, your body is speaking to you. What it's speaking to you about is your life. You'll find that there is a correlation between where your body hurts or is too fat and what's going on in your life. In order to change your body, you have to take care of your body and your life simultaneously.

**Example**

Your stomach represents your intuition, "gut reaction," and your ability to digest new ideas. It also has to do with the flow of ideas. When you experience problems such as stomach cramps, or a buildup of extra weight, there is a blockage in your life. You may be feeling trapped, stuck, or unable to move in or out of a certain situation. You may be listening to your mind chatter and not following your intuition.

Appendix A, *Body Parts and Affirmations*, lists all the parts of your body and what they mean in your life. These meanings are windows. They give you an opportunity to look more closely at your life, decide what is or isn't working, and then do something about it. Next to each meaning is an affirmation designed to help you begin the process of turning your life around. Remember, before the change can occur you have to change your thinking; first comes the thought, then comes the change. As you turn your life around, your body won't have to continue giving you warning messages and can begin its own process of turning around.

## What Is Your Body Saying?

What part or aspect of your body is bothering you most? Take a look at Appendix A and see what that part represents in your life.

**Example**

*Body part or aspect:*   I have gained 10 pounds in the last few months. The weight has settled in my upper arms, hips, buttocks, and thighs.

Your turn: _____

_____

_____

## What It Means

*Fat, or excess weight*, represents fear. It is the body's way of protecting itself. Fear can be caused by feelings of helplessness or instability. Fat can also represent denial or fear of one's own feelings. The more overweight one becomes, the deeper the feelings are buried. Fat can also be a mechanism for covering over feelings of powerlessness, anger, rage, disappointment, and sadness.

*Upper arms* represent the capacity to embrace all that life has to offer. They represent joy, discouragement, or fear. Fat or pain in your upper arms may mean you are holding yourself back from experiencing life fully.

Your *hips and pelvic area* represent balance, movement, and creativity. If you have extra weight or problems in your hips, your life may be

**8**

out of balance, or you may be overloaded in one area (for example, work versus play). Your hips also symbolize your relationship with creativity and sexuality. If you have a pain in your hips, you may want to look at how you are failing to express yourself in those areas.

Your *buttocks* are the seat of power. When you have too much or too little weight on the buttocks, it usually means fear of your own or someone else's power. It also has to do with whether you are willing to own your own power. When the buttocks are out of shape, power is mishandled or loosely held. The buttocks are also the center of all motion. When there is pain in the buttocks, power is blocked.

Your *thighs* represent strength and forward motion. Excess weight on the thighs may mean you are clinging to the past and beliefs from childhood, which are holding you back. These childhood beliefs are often associated with anger, fear, rage, and powerlessness. Having excess weight on the thighs may mean you are not able to express anger or you feel impotent in your anger. Excess weight and pain in your thighs may indicate an inability to move forward in your life.

What is your body telling you? _____

_____

_____

_____

_____

_____

_____

_____

_____

_____

*Note:* If you run out of space, continue exploring your body messages in your journal.

## What It Means to You

Now that you've read what each of the body parts you're dealing with means, take a moment to figure out what your body could be telling you. Look at your life in relationship to the information you just received.

### Example

> *Excess weight:* I have spent the last eight months traveling. I feel unsettled and slightly unstable.

*Upper arms:*  I'm sometimes afraid of what's coming in my life. I have never experienced being so "on the edge" with my home and my work.

*Buttocks:*  I am very powerful as a teacher and "change maker." I'm sometimes afraid that if others see my power they will be put off; they may not like me.

*Hips:*  I haven't been expressing my creativity during the past eight months. The book I am writing now was in its gestation period. Now that I'm writing, maybe the weight will come off my hips.

*Thighs*:  I still have the fear of not being enough. Sometimes I also fear the speed with which I'm moving forward in my life. I also get angry that things don't happen fast enough for me.

Your turn: _____

_____

_____

_____

_____

_____

_____

_____

_____

_____

_____

## Putting It All Together

Take a look at all the things that your body is telling you. What needs to happen in your life so that your body can stop sending you the messages it's sending?

### Example

I need to *know* that I am safe living my life the way I'm living it.

I need to *know* I am secure no matter where I am, and that I'm going to be okay in all the new situations and experiences that are coming to me.

I also need to *know* that it's okay for me to be powerful and to move forward in my life quickly.

And finally, I need to *know* that everything I need is coming to me at the right time.

Your turn: _____

_____

_____

_____

_____

_____

_____

_____

_____

_____

## What Has to Change?

What has to change in yourself in order for you to have what you want in your life?

### Example

> I have to stop being afraid I won't ever have a place to live again.
>
> I have to stop being afraid of what's coming in my life (I'm only afraid of what I cannot see).
>
> I have to stop being afraid of being powerful.

Your turn: _____

_____

_____

_____

_____

_____

_____

_____

_____

When you begin to change your life or the fears you have about your life, you will begin to easily and effortlessly change what isn't working in your body. I have been through this process several times with my body, and it always works . . . as long as I'm working it.

You now know what your body is telling you about your life. Tomorrow you will learn how to develop affirmations to begin the process of change.

## DAILY EXERCISES

### Becoming Aware Exercise

Continue to notice how you feel after you eat. Write your observations in your food diary.

### Physical Exercises

Continue the exercise program from Days 5–7 and add the following exercises.

# 29 TRICEP PRESS (arms)

Stand with your feet hip width apart and relax your shoulders. Tighten your buttocks and abdominals and tuck your buttocks under in a slight C curve. With a 1- or 2-pound barbell in each hand, bend forward slightly from your hips, as you bend your elbows back and place your hands at your waist with your wrists facing forward. Pull your shoulder blades together toward your spine. Exhale and press both arms straight back. Inhale and bend your elbows, returning your hands to your waist. Repeat 12 times and rest 30 seconds. Do 2 sets of 12 repetitions, resting 30 seconds between sets, as you repeat the affirmations for arms.

**AFFIRMATIONS FOR ARMS**

*I love my beautiful arms. They are strong, toned, and well defined. I embrace my life with joy and ease. I welcome new experiences in life with delight. I am safe embracing all that comes to me in my life. I love my life and all it has to offer me.*

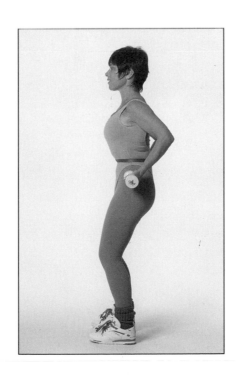

8

Bend forward and place your right knee and right hand on a chair or bench. Keep your left leg straight with the knee soft. Hold a barbell in your left hand and allow your arm to dangle down from your shoulder. Turn your arm so that your hand faces forward and your elbow back. Exhale and bend the elbow of your left arm up. Continue to exhale as you straighten your arm up and behind you. Inhale and bend your arm. Continue to inhale as you slowly lower your arm to the original position.

Repeat 12 times and change arms. Do 12 with your right hand. Repeat series twice as you say the affirmations for arms in Exercise 29.

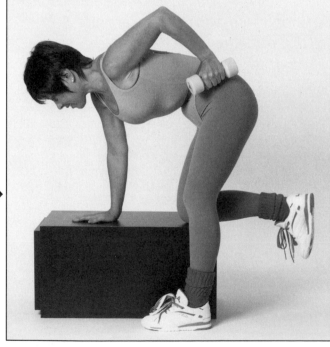

8

Stand with your feet hip width apart. Tighten your buttocks and abdominals, and tuck your buttocks under in a slight C curve. Take a barbell in each hand and hold them together over your head. Be sure your buttocks are tucked under so that your lower spine is protected by the C curve. Keeping your arms over your head, and your upper arms close to your ears, elbows upright, inhale and lower your forearms back behind you. Exhale and raise them up again. Repeat 12 times and rest 30 seconds. Do 2 sets of 12 repetitions, resting 30 seconds between sets, as you say the affirmations for arms in Exercise 29.

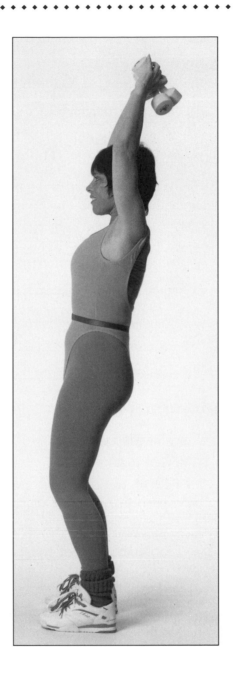
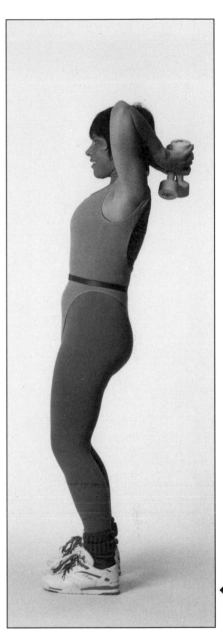

## Mind Chatter Turnarounds

In your journal, write down all the negative things your mind told you while you were exercising and turn them around. You don't have to limit this exercise to body issues. Relationships, money, lifestyle, sex, children, and work are some of the things that may push themselves into your mind as you exercise.

### Affirmation Exercise

Create an affirmation for today as described on pages 70–76. Write it down in your journal and be sure to look at it every once in a while during the day.

### Visualization Exercise

Create a visualization for your affirmation as described on pages 107–108.

### Today's Nurture

Look over your nurtures list on page 115, add more if you've thought of more, and choose one. Make sure you give it to yourself by the end of the day.

*Make your appointment with yourself for tomorrow:*

Name: _____

Date: _____

Book time: _____

Exercise time: _____

## EVENING PROCESS

Review your goal.

Review today's tasks.

Check off those you have accomplished.

Carry over to tomorrow anything you didn't finish today.

### Ten End-of-the-Day Acknowledgments

1. _____
2. _____
3. _____
4. _____
5. _____
6. _____
7. _____
8. _____
9. _____
10. _____

8

DAY
9

## AFFIRMATIONS FOR BODY PARTS

Restate the goal as set for you on Day 1 and your personal goal.

_____

_____

_____

_____

Review and restate today's tasks: _____

_____

_____

_____

_____

On Day 5 you wrote your tasks through Day 9. Now that you have a better handle on what you're asking of yourself, write the tasks for Days 10 through 13.

Day 10: _____

_____

_____

_____

_____

Day 11: _____

_____

_____

_____

Day 12: _____

_____

_____

_____

_____

Day 13: _____

_____

_____

_____

_____

In Appendix A, following each body part and what it represents, are several affirmations. Basically, they are turnarounds—positive statements about the part of your life that the body part represents. They are also positive statements about the body part itself. Here's where you begin to subconsciously change your body and your life.

I learned a trick several years ago. The trick was to find positive value in a negative situation. I have written many of my affirmations from that point of view. For example, I used to have an adversarial relationship with my rear end. I only saw how fat it was. To change my relationship with it, I had to begin seeing its positive points. Physically I couldn't see them yet, so I started from a different direction: I began telling myself only wonderful things about my rear. I said, "I love my rear end. It's loyal. I always know where to find it. It follows me wherever I go. It cushions me if I sit down too hard. It fills out my pants with a distinctive line, and it will protect me in case of famine." Now, who could get mad at a rear end like that? The interesting thing here is that I not only ended my adversarial relationship with my rear, but it has become more attractive.

Let's look at the parts of your body (life) that are not working for you right now.

## Example
I have excess weight on my upper arms, hips, buttocks, and thighs.

Your turn: _____

_____

What are some affirmations that could go with each of these areas?

*Excess weight or fat:*   I love my fat. It has always protected me and kept me safe. It has done a great job and now it can go on vacation permanently. I am safe in every feeling and every aspect of my life.

*Upper arms:* My upper arms are beautiful, strong, toned, and firm. I lovingly hold and embrace my life's experiences.

*Buttocks:* I love my buttocks. They are firm, toned, strong, and beautiful. I am safe in my power and use it wisely and with love.

*Hips:* My hips are perfect, strong, toned, shapely, and flexible. I am free to move forward, in perfect balance and with joy and laughter. I express my creativity and my sexuality with ease and joy.

*Thighs:* My thighs are beautiful, strong, toned, and well defined. They move forward with grace and ease. I forgive all childhood trespasses, real and imagined. I love life, release all fear, and enjoy my past and present experiences.

## Create an Affirmation

Look at yesterday's exercise where you put together all the information your body gave you. You should have a list of body parts and a list of things they represent in your life. In the space provided below, write affirmations that go with the body parts you want to work on (either copy them or make up your own). If you run out of space, continue the exercise in your journal.

Body part: _____

Affirmation: _____

_____

_____

_____

_____

_____

_____

_____

_____

Copy this affirmation onto a separate piece of paper and put it somewhere where you will see it often during the day.

## DAILY EXERCISES

### Becoming Aware Exercise

Continue to notice how you feel after you eat. Write your observations in your food diary.

Continue the exercise program from Days 5–8 and add the following exercises.

# 32 ARM RAISES (shoulders)

· · · · · · · · · · · · · · · · · · · · · · · · · · · · · · · · · · · · · · · · · · · · · · · · · · · · · · · · · · · · ·

Stand with your feet hip width apart; relax your shoulders. Tighten your buttocks and abdominals, and tuck your buttocks under in a slight C curve. Hold a 1- or 2-pound barbell in each hand, with your hands facing your body and your elbows relaxed (your arms slightly bent). Exhale and raise your right arm straight up in front of you to shoulder height. Inhale and slowly lower your arm to its original position. Remember to maintain control as you lower your arm. Repeat 12 times and change arms. Repeat 12 times with the left arm. As you do 2 sets of 12 repetitions with each arm, be sure you say the affirmations for shoulders.

---

**AFFIRMATIONS FOR SHOULDERS**

*I love my shoulders. My shoulders are beautiful. They are strong, straight, and lovely to look at. I carry my life with ease. My burdens become lighter with every passing day. I love my life and all my responsibilities. They are easy to handle and joyful to experience. I love my life.*

---

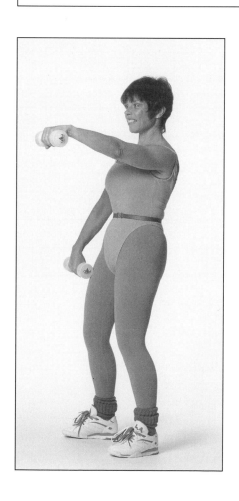

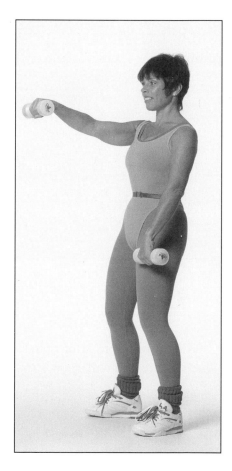

9

# 33 LATERAL RAISES (shoulders)

Stand with your feet hip width apart; relax your shoulders. Tighten your buttocks and abdominals and tuck your buttocks under in a slight C curve. Hold a 1- or 2-pound barbell in each hand with your hands resting straight down at your sides, wrists facing in toward your thighs. Relax your elbows so that your arms bend slightly. Exhale and raise both arms out to your sides to shoulder height. Inhale and slowly lower your arms to their original position. Be sure you maintain control as you lower your arms. Repeat 12 times and rest 30 seconds. Do 2 sets of 12 repetitions. Be sure you rest 30 seconds between sets. Repeat affirmations for shoulders (see Exercise 32).

# 34 UPRIGHT ROWS (shoulders)

Stand with your feet hip width apart. Tighten your buttocks and abdominals, and tuck your buttocks under in a slight C curve. Holding a barbell in each hand, place your hands close together in front of you. Keep your hands close together and elbows out to your sides. Exhale as you lift the barbells toward your chin; your elbows should thrust outward. Inhale and slowly lower your hands to their original position. Be sure to maintain control as you slowly lower your hands. Repeat 12 times and rest 30 seconds. Do 2 sets of 12 repetitions, making sure you rest 30 seconds between sets. Repeat the affirmations for shoulders (see Exercise 32).

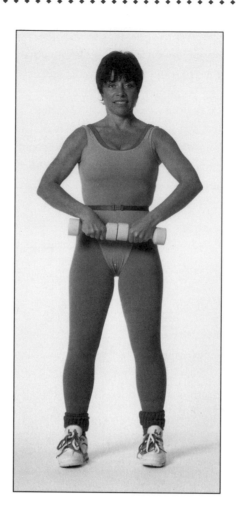 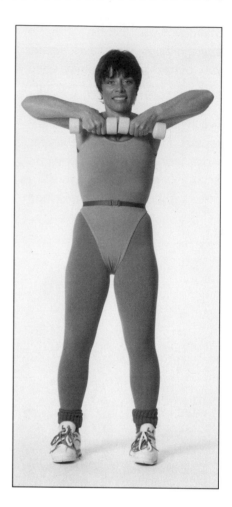

## Mind Chatter Turnarounds

Write down in your journal all the negative things your mind told you while you were exercising and turn them around.

## Affirmation Exercise

Create an affirmation for today as described on pages 70–71. Write it down in your journal and be sure to look at it every once in a while during the day.

## Visualization Exercise

Create a visualization for your affirmation as described on pages 107–108.

9

## Today's Nurture

Look over your nurtures list on page 115, add more if you've thought of more, and choose one. Make sure you give it to yourself by the end of the day.

*Make your appointment with yourself for tomorrow:*

Name: _____

Date: _____

Book time: _____

Exercise time: _____

## EVENING PROCESS

Review your goal.

Review today's tasks.

Check off those you have accomplished.

Carry over to tomorrow anything you didn't finish today.

### Ten End-of-the-Day Acknowledgments

1. _____
2. _____
3. _____
4. _____
5. _____
6. _____
7. _____
8. _____
9. _____
10. _____

9

*Truth is tough.*

Oliver Wendell Holmes, Sr.
*The Autocrat of the Breakfast-Table*

## TELLING THE TRUTH

Restate the goal as set for you on Day 1 and your personal goal.

_____

_____

_____

_____

Review and restate today's tasks: _____

_____

_____

_____

_____

_____

_____

For me, telling the truth to and about myself is the single hardest thing I ever have or have had to do. Telling the truth has *nothing* to do with lying. Telling the truth has nothing to do with any person other than yourself.

An example of telling the truth:

A friend asks you to go to the movies. You don't want to go. The truthful answer is "No." That's the truth. When was the last time someone asked you to the movies and you simply said "No" or "No, thank you." Not "I'm busy tonight." Not "I have to take the kids to Cub Scouts." Not "I don't feel well." Just "No, thank you," with no explanation?

It has been my experience that when it comes to eating it's almost impossible to tell the truth. Have you ever noticed that if you say "No, thank you" to someone who is offering you food, he or she wants to know

"Why not?" And if you have no reason, other than you just don't want it, he or she tries to convince you to eat it?

A variation on the theme of not telling the truth occurs when you don't even tell *yourself* that you don't want something. This is known as denial. An example of denial: You decide not to eat any more junk food. You go downtown. You get hungry. You see a junk food store. You start to salivate and you say to yourself, "It's okay. I worked hard today. One little bit won't hurt. I'll start tomorrow." This type of denial is particularly prevalent before you make any major changes in your life, like going on a diet, starting an exercise program, or beginning a budget plan—anything the mind can interpret as future deprivation.

The trick to telling the truth is being consistently honest. If you keep telling yourself you're in good enough shape when you can't bend over and touch the floor, walk six blocks, or do six sit-ups, you're not telling yourself the truth about yourself. If you want to lose 10 pounds and you eat foods that are heavy in fat and sugar while telling yourself you're not, or saying to yourself "All I have to do is look at food and I put weight on," while you nibble constantly here and there, you're not telling the truth. ("All I have to do is look at food and I put on weight" is an affirmation. You may want to stop saying it.) So the trick to telling the truth is telling the truth.

Telling the truth is not about passing judgment on other people. "You look awful" is not telling the truth, it's a judgment. And a judgment is an opinion, it is not necessarily the truth. Sharing your judgments (the truth as you see it) about other people with them now that you've decided to tell the truth is not such a good idea. Telling the truth about *yourself* is all you can do. You will find it challenging enough.

How do you tell the truth? The first step is to be aware of what you really want. Do you want to change your body? Does changing your body mean you have to eat more carefully? Does it mean you need more exercise? You see, if you've been saying that you're on a diet and you haven't lost a pound, you've not been telling the truth from two points of view. The first and most important is that you're really not on a diet. The second, and more subtle, is that you probably don't *want* to be on a diet. If you wanted to be on a diet you would be on a diet, and if you were on a diet you'd lose weight. Your results are your teacher and you can't fool your body.

There's only one way to tell the truth and that's to tell it, but first you have to know what you want. And sometimes you have to train the people around you, particularly those who love you, to hear the truth.

If your mother has been used to feeding you a lot, perhaps that's her way of showing love. You might have to have a conversation with her. Such a conversation might sound like:

"I have to cut down on my eating. I don't always feel comfortable saying no to you. I need your help in cutting back. Is it okay to say no to you if I've had enough to eat?" Don't be surprised if your mother sees this as a putdown. Remind her that it's not about her, it's not about her cooking, it's simply your truth about yourself. Tell her you love her and stick to your guns.

**10**

## Telling the Truth Exercise

Think of three examples of times you did not tell the truth.

**Example**

I told myself I was going to start exercising, but I still haven't. I ate dessert when I didn't want it because I didn't want to hurt my sister's boyfriend's feelings when he offered it to me.

Your turn: _____

_____

_____

_____

Now, what could you do differently under similar circumstances in the future?

**Example**

I could start my exercise program when I say I will, now. I could politely refuse the dessert and stick with my decision.

Your turn: _____

_____

_____

_____

Notice what you say you're going to do and whether or not you do it. Notice how many times you do and don't tell the truth. Each day you will write down where you didn't tell the truth until you become so conscious of it you won't do anything but tell the truth. Awareness is the first step.

## DAILY EXERCISES

### Becoming Aware Exercise

Continue to notice how you feel after you eat. Write your observations in your food diary.

### Physical Exercises

Continue your exercise program from Days 5–9 and add the following exercises.

# 35 SHOULDER STRETCH (shoulders)

Stand with your feet hip width apart, shoulders relaxed. Tighten your buttocks and abdominals, and tuck your buttocks under in a slight C curve. Cross your right arm in front of your chest. Place your left hand on the upper right arm and, keeping your shoulders relaxed and lowered, press your right arm close to your chest, stretching the shoulder muscles. Hold 10 to 20 seconds while you say the shoulder affirmations and release. Change sides and do the same with your left arm.

### AFFIRMATIONS FOR SHOULDERS

*My shoulders are perfect, strong, straight, and very beautiful. I love my life and carry my responsibilities lightly. I follow through easily on all that I do. Life is fun.*

# 36 TRICEP STRETCH (arms)

Stand with your feet hip width apart, shoulders relaxed. Tighten your buttocks and abdominals, and tuck your buttocks under in a slight C curve. Raise your right arm straight up, bend it, and place your right hand between your shoulder blades. Take your left hand and place it on your right arm near your elbow. Gently pull your right arm back behind your head or as far as possible. Hold 10 to 20 seconds while you say the affirmations for arms and release. Change arms and repeat.

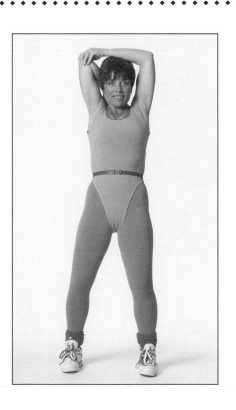

### AFFIRMATIONS FOR ARMS

*I love my arms. They are beautiful, strong, and well defined. I embrace life with joy. I am safe in all of life's experiences.*

**10**

# 37 CHEST STRETCH (chest and upper back)

Stand with your feet hip width apart, shoulders relaxed. Tighten your buttocks and abdominals. Tuck your buttocks under in a slight C curve. Clasp your hands behind your back with your fingers laced and your palms facing your body. Raise both arms up behind you as far as you can, and hold 10 to 20 seconds as you say the affirmations.

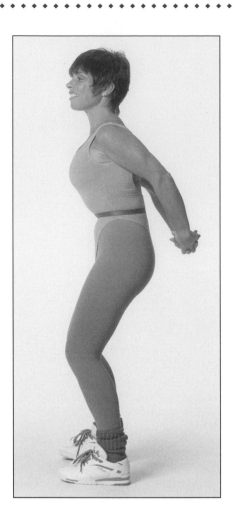

## AFFIRMATIONS FOR CHEST AND UPPER BACK

**Chest:** *My chest is beautiful. I love life. I am safe giving and receiving love. I nurture myself and others with joy.*
**Back:** *I have a beautiful, strong, and healthy back. It is safe for me to love and to be loved. I am supported by life. All my needs and desires are met in present time.*

## Mind Chatter Turnarounds

Write down in your journal all the negative things your mind told you while you were exercising and turn them around.

## Affirmation Exercise

Create an affirmation for today as described on pages 70–71. Write it down in your journal and be sure to refer to it during the day.

## Visualization Exercise

Create a visualization for your affirmation as described on pages 107–108.

## What Is Your Body Saying Today?

Continue to look at your body and ask yourself how it feels. Look up the areas of discomfort in Appendix A, interpret what they mean, and create an affirmation to turn the feelings around. Create an affirmation that addresses what your body tells you, or use one from Appendix A.

## Today's Nurture

Look over your nurtures list on page 115, add more if you've thought of more, and choose one to give to yourself today.

*Make your appointment with yourself for tomorrow:*

Name: _____

Date: _____

Book time: _____

Exercise time: _____

## EVENING PROCESS

Review your goal.

Review today's tasks.

Check off those you have accomplished.

Carry over to tomorrow anything you didn't finish today.

### Ten End-of-the-Day Acknowledgments

1. _____

2. _____

3. _____

4. _____

5. _____

6. _____

7. _____

8. _____

9. _____

10. _____

**10**

## ASK YOUR BODY WHAT IT WANTS

Restate the goal as set for you on Day 1 and your personal goal.

_____

_____

_____

_____

_____

Review and restate today's tasks: _____

_____

_____

_____

_____

_____

_____

_____

After all the weird things you've been doing for the past 10 days, talking to your body shouldn't come as a great surprise. What might come as a surprise is getting some answers. Just as your body knows when it's hungry, tired, or satisfied, it knows what it wants and what it doesn't want.

You are questioning and getting responses from your body all the time, even though you may not know that's what you've been doing. For example, when you go out for dinner and make your decision about what you want to eat, it is your body that tells you. You may think it's your brain, but where do you think your brain got its information?

The trouble comes when your Aunt Mathilda makes the decision. If your body tells you it wants a salad, and Aunt Mathilda tells you to eat steak, and you eat steak, you deny the body. Chances are the steak will not sit as well as the salad would have. (Once you're out of whack, Aunt Mathilda will force dessert on you and then you're really in trouble.)

One night my sister Joan and I went out with friends for after-dinner cappuccino. When we got to the restaurant, I kept having the feeling I wanted spinach. It was 11:30 at night and my spinach craving seemed ridiculous. The longer I sat there, the more I wanted the spinach. My friends kept offering alternative solutions: apple pie, cheesecake, carrot cake, ice cream—anything but spinach. They couldn't understand how anyone could want to eat spinach with her cappuccino, and frankly, neither could I. I think they were embarrassed to be sitting at a table with someone eating spinach with cappuccino. But that's what I wanted, and that's what I ordered . . . three orders.

Whatever was going on, my body was absolutely satisfied by the spinach. If I had ordered something else, the craving wouldn't have been satisfied, and I would have made myself ill. Your body asks for things all the time. You have to retrain yourself to listen.

Just as your body lets you know what it wants, it also lets you know what it doesn't want.

**Example**

I was very hungry. I was returning from a business trip, it was late afternoon, and I hadn't eaten all day. I stopped and got a sandwich at a health food store on my way home. Fifteen minutes later, while I was filling my car with gas, I decided to get a candy bar. My body said, "No." My response was, "What do you mean, no? You like candy." My body said, "Not today."

I said, "But I have candy all the time; I tell people they can eat whatever they want."

"That's right, you do, and today I don't want candy!"

"But I'm bored pumping gas. I want to eat a candy bar."

"Boredom is not a reason for eating what I don't want."

I ate the candy bar. Three guesses what happened. My body punished me ever so slightly by becoming nauseated for the next four hours. The conversation on the rest of the drive home went like this:

"I told you I didn't want it."

"Yes, but I thought you were wrong."

"I'm never wrong."

Practice talking to your body (you may want to do this silently). If you ask your body what it wants, it will tell you. Then it's up to you whether you follow its directions. But be careful. You might confuse your body's voice with mind chatter, especially if you're not used to listening to it. If your body constantly tells you to eat food you know is junk, it's not your body talking. You have to be conscious of what is real and what is not—you know the difference. This process is about telling the truth . . . to yourself. Write down what your body is telling you today.

**Example**

My body needs to exercise every two hours during this writing process. My body needs to eat protein today. My body needs to go for a walk.

Your turn: What is your body telling you today? _____

_____

_____

_____

_____

_____

You can discover what your body wants and needs simply by asking it. I do this by saying, "What do you want?" My body will reply. The trick is hearing it, and that takes practice.

## DAILY EXERCISES

### Becoming Aware Exercise

Continue to notice how you feel after you eat. Write your observations in your food diary.

### Physical Exercises

Continue your exercise program from Days 5–10 and add the following exercises.

# 38 SQUATS (buttocks)

With a 1- or 2-pound barbell in each hand, stand with your feet wider than hip width apart, knees soft, shoulders relaxed. Tighten your buttocks and abdominals. Place your hands by your hips. Hold your chest upright and inhale as you slowly squat down as if you were about to sit in a chair. Your thighs should be parallel to the floor when squatting. Exhale and stand straight again. Repeat 12 times and rest 30 seconds. Do one more set of 12 and say the affirmations for buttocks.

## AFFIRMATIONS FOR BUTTOCKS

*I love my buttocks. I have a beautiful rear end. I am safe with my power and with the power of others. I use my power wisely and with love. I look great in pants.*

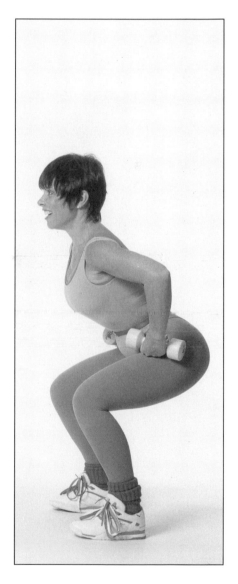

# 39 LUNGES (buttocks)

• • • • • • • • • • • • • • • • • • • • • • • • • • • • • • • • • • • • • • • • • • • • • •

With a 1- or 2-pound weight in each hand, stand with your feet together, knees soft, shoulders relaxed. Tighten your buttocks and abdominals. Place your hands at your sides. Exhale and lunge forward with your right foot, bending your right knee, and dipping your left knee toward the floor. Your right knee should be over your ankle. Inhale and return to standing position. Exhale and lunge forward with your left foot, bending your left knee, and dipping your right knee toward the floor. Your left knee should be over your ankle. Inhale and return to standing position.

Alternating legs, repeat 12 times and rest 30 seconds. Do a second set of 12 and say the affirmations for buttocks in Exercise 38.

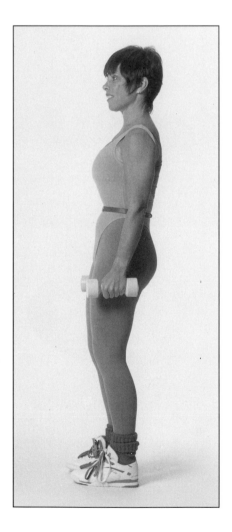

# 40 STEP UP (buttocks)

With a 1- or 2-pound weight in each hand, face a bench or a step and stand with feet together, knees soft, shoulders relaxed. Tighten your buttocks and abdominals. Place your hands by your hips. Exhale and step up onto the bench or step with your right foot. Inhale and step down again. Be sure to maintain control at all times. Exhale and step up onto the bench or step with your left foot. Inhale and step down again, maintaining control. Repeat 12 times and rest 30 seconds. Do another set of 12 and say the affirmations for buttocks in Exercise 38.

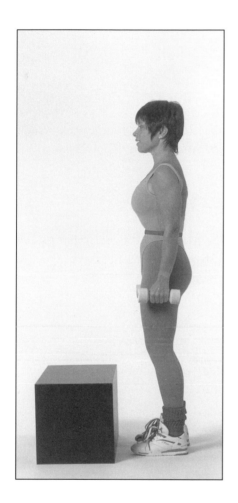

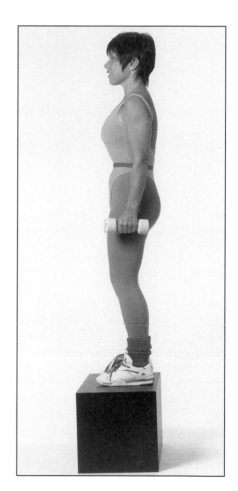

## Mind Chatter Turnarounds

In your journal, write down all the negative things your mind told you while you were exercising and turn them around.

## Affirmation Exercise

Create an affirmation for today as described on pages 70–71. Write it down in your journal and be sure to refer to it during the day.

## Visualization Exercise

Create a visualization for your affirmation as described on pages 107–108.

## What Is Your Body Saying Today?

Ask your body how it feels. Write your observations in your journal. Look up what the itches, aches, and pains mean in Appendix A.

## Today's Nurture

Look over your nurtures list on page 115, add more if you've thought of more, and choose one to give to yourself by the end of the day.

## Telling the Truth Exercise

Think of three opportunities you had for telling yourself the truth today. What can you do differently under similar circumstances in the future? Create an affirmation that you think will help you tell yourself the truth.

## Affirmations

Create an affirmation for the body part that's bothering you, or use one from Appendix A.

*Make your appointment with yourself for tomorrow:*

Name: _____

Date: _____

Book time: _____

Exercise time: _____

## EVENING PROCESS

Look at your goal.

Review today's tasks.

Check off those you have accomplished.

Carry over to tomorrow anything you didn't finish today.

### Ten End-of-the-Day Acknowledgments

1. _____

2. _____

3. _____

4. _____

5. _____

6. _____

7. _____

8. _____

9. _____

10. _____

## SELF-ACCEPTANCE

Restate the goal as set for you on Day 1 and your personal goal.

_____

_____

_____

_____

Review and restate today's tasks: _____

_____

_____

_____

_____

_____

    This exercise is about ownership—self-ownership. I've found that I used to simply ignore, or deny, the parts of myself I didn't like or didn't want. It was as if they didn't exist for me. But how can you change something that doesn't exist? Resistance is another form of lack of ownership, and what you resist persists. As I said in Chapter 1, the key to change is self-acceptance. It is easy to accept the parts you like; it's harder to accept the things you don't like about yourself.

    When I first started to study metaphysics and mind control, I took a course in New York with June Graham and Jim Spencer called "Let Go and Live." I had no idea what I was getting into when I signed up. The course taught how to love the parts of yourself that you resisted. During the first day I discovered that the part of myself I resisted most, at that time, was being stupid. I had been called stupid most of my life and I *refused* to accept it. One of the workshop exercises was to create a character that represented the part of ourselves we didn't like. I created Gracie. Gracie is adorably stupid.

Next we were told to take this character home with us and make peace with it. I found this exercise very scary. I did not want to be stupid but I did want to heal, so I let Gracie be stupid. Every time I did something I judged to be stupid, I turned to Gracie, who sat on my shoulder, and said, "Look what we did. Boy, are we stupid!" And we would laugh together. To my surprise, I began to enjoy being stupid. It was funny. It became okay. As it became more okay, it seemed I made fewer gaffes.

About two months after I met Gracie, I noticed George. I was at a luncheon interview for a magazine. The interview was finished before the lunch was, so the interviewer and I began to talk politics. I can't remember exactly what was said, but the interviewer stopped me and asked, "Where did you learn this?" I told him the truth. I said, "I made it up." He said, "It's brilliant." That's when I met George. He now sits on my other shoulder and pontificates.

What I learned was that in order for me to experience George, my brilliance, I had to make peace with Gracie, my stupidity. If I had been worried about appearing stupid during the conversation that followed the interview, I would have been too afraid to risk displaying my own intelligence.

We are both sides of a coin and we have to own each of them in order to experience either of them.

The trick is to own what you don't like about yourself. Not just own it, accept it. Have fun with it. Defuse it.

## Character Exercise

Write down one thing that disturbs you about yourself. Choose the thing that really grates on you.

**Example**
My client Ellen is distressed that when she looks in the mirror, she sees a whale.

Your turn: _____

_____

Now create a character to represent that quality.

**Example**
Ellen created a happy, singing whale, like Widgy the Singing Whale, who used to be on a record she listened to as a child. She calls her whale Widgy.

Your turn: _____

_____

Now take that character wherever you go and develop a positive relationship with it. Talk to it. Laugh with it. Be thoughtful with it. Learn from it.

During her conversations with Widgy, Ellen discovered that Widgy's greatest fear was not being able to eat whatever he wanted. Sometimes Widgy would say, "I know if I want to be thin, I will never be able to eat certain things again." In anticipation of deprivation, Widgy consistently overate. What Ellen had to do was to reassure Widgy that he could eat everything he wanted but that he had to be smart about it. He could eat because he was hungry, not because he was crazed. This was a totally new concept to Widgy, and as Ellen practiced being smart, Widgy calmed down and didn't have to eat everything in sight.

Let's talk for a moment about addiction. People who overeat are addicted to food. People who don't agree with that statement aren't looking honestly at what's going on. Any time anything controls your actions it's an addiction. The operational word is *controls*.

The way most people deal with their addictions is abstinence. There are certain foods that members of Overeaters Anonymous never eat. I have a client who in the past couldn't accept invitations to dinner because he might be confronted with a food he knew he shouldn't eat but couldn't resist. The food was still in control. That's an extreme, but it does happen. Some people want to be able to live sensibly with their addictions. They want to be able to eat whatever they want without the food taking control. In the beginning, that's much harder than abstinence, but in the long run it keeps the ups and downs from happening. You can't fall off a wagon if you're never on one.

If I eat three meals a day, plus dessert, no matter how I feel—that's addiction. If, on the other hand, I eat when I'm hungry and stop when I'm satisfied, even before dessert, that's power.

Ellen found she had to teach Widgy how to be powerful. As Widgy became more powerful, so did Ellen. She has begun the process of being smart around food. It no longer controls her. But first, she had to make peace with Widgy.

You have created a character to represent what you don't like about yourself. I cannot tell you what your character needs. In my case, making peace with Gracie allowed George to emerge. In Ellen's case, empowering Widgy allowed Ellen to become powerful and smart around food. Spend time with your character and find out what it needs.

## Character Dialogue

If you need more space for this exercise, use your journal.

What did your character say to you today? _____

_____

What does it need? _____

_____

What does it want? _____

_____

If you don't hear anything in the beginning, that's okay; you will eventually. Remember, this part of you has been ignored or hated for a long time. It may take a while to communicate. Keep asking and you will get your answers.

## DAILY EXERCISES

### Becoming Aware Exercise

Continue to notice how you feel after you eat and write your observations in your food diary.

### What Does Your Body Want?

Ask your body what it wants to eat today. Ask your body how it wants to move today. Write any unusual answers in your journal. Be sure to give your body what it wants.

### Physical Exercises

Continue your exercise program from Days 5–11 and add the following exercises.

# 41 ROUND AND STRAIGHTEN (lower abdominals)

Sit with your knees bent and your feet flat on the floor. Tuck your pelvis under in a slight C curve. Breathe normally. Grasp your thighs under your knees, press your spine forward and upward, and relax your shoulders. Tighten your abdominals and slowly round your spine. Inhale and lower your torso slightly backward to the count of 4. Be sure to keep your shoulders relaxed.

Hold the rounded position for 4 counts, then release your abdominal muscles. Tighten your abdominals again and exhale as you slowly straighten your spine, sitting up to the count of 4. Hold the upright position for the count of 4 (keep breathing), then release your abdominal muscles. Repeat the entire exercise 6 times as you say the affirmations for abdominals.

### AFFIRMATIONS FOR ABDOMINALS

*I love my stomach. It is strong, well defined, and very beautiful. I digest new ideas with ease. It is easy for me to understand how much I know. I move forward in my life knowing I am safe and that all is well in my world. My abdominal muscles love to exercise.*

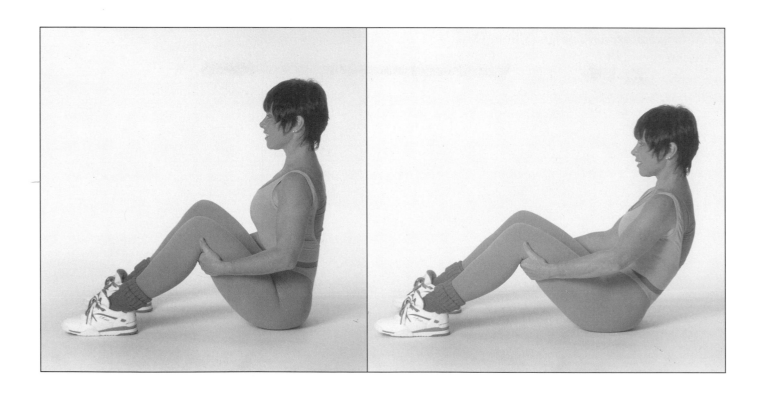

**LOWER ABDOMINAL CURL** (lower abdominals)

Lie on your back, knees bent, feet flat on the floor. Tuck your pelvis under in a slight C curve. Place one hand against the side of your buttocks so you can feel their movement, and one hand on your lower abdominals just above the pubic bone.

Exhale as you tighten your lower abdominals *only* and lift your relaxed buttocks slightly off the floor. Using your hands, check to see whether your abdominals are working and your buttocks are relaxed. Inhale as you then release. Repeat the curl 16 times as you say the affirmations for abdominals in Exercise 41.

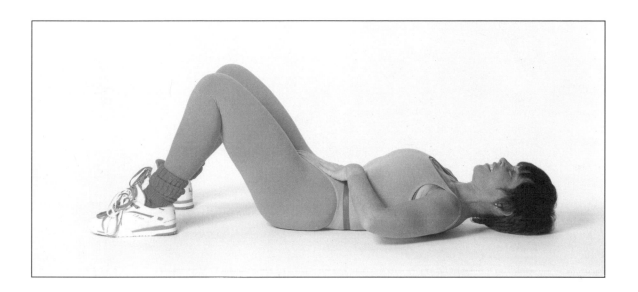

# 43 LOWER ABDOMINAL CURL, KNEES UP (lower abdominals)

Lie on your back, knees bent, feet flat on the floor, arms at your sides. Tuck your pelvis under in a slight C curve. Lift your feet off the floor, bending your knees over your chest. Keep your heels as low as possible. Keeping your legs as still as possible, exhale and lift your buttocks off the floor. Inhale and lower. Repeat 16 times as you say the affirmations for abdominals in Exercise 41.

## Mind Chatter Turnarounds

In your journal, write down all the negative things your mind told you while you were exercising and turn them around.

## Affirmation Exercise

Create an affirmation for today as described on pages 70–71. Write it down in your journal and be sure to refer to it during the day.

## Visualization Exercise

Create a visualization for your affirmation as described on pages 107–108.

## What Is Your Body Saying Today?

Ask your body how it feels today. Write down the areas you are having problems with and interpret what they mean to you. Look up the affirmations in Appendix A and select one for today, or create one that works for you.

## Today's Nurture

Look over your nurtures list on page 115, add more if you've thought of more, and choose one. Make sure you give it to yourself by the end of the day.

## Telling the Truth Exercise

Ask yourself and your body whether you are telling the truth about the progress you are making with this program. If you feel you are off, what has to happen to get you to tell the truth? Write your answer in your journal.

*Make your appointment with yourself for tomorrow:*

Name: _____

Date: _____

Book time: _____

Exercise time: _____

## EVENING PROCESS

Review your goal.

Review today's tasks.

Check off those you have accomplished.

Look back at the "What Does Your Body Want?" exercise.

Did you give it what it wants today? If not, what has to change? Write the answer in your journal.

## Ten End-of-the-Day Acknowledgments

1. _____

2. _____

3. _____

4. _____

5. _____

6. _____

7. _____

8. _____

9. _____

10. _____

## TREASURE MAPPING

Restate the goal as set for you on Day 1 and your personal goal.

_____

_____

_____

_____

Review and restate today's tasks: _____

_____

_____

_____

_____

_____

Write tasks for Days 14–17:

Day 14: _____

_____

_____

_____

_____

Day 15: _____

_____

_____

_____

_____

Day 16: _____

_____

_____

_____

_____

Day 17: _____

_____

_____

_____

_____

Treasure mapping is one of my favorite exercises. It is a creative way of picturing things the way you want them to be. A treasure map is a collage of whatever it is you want: a home, money, a relationship, a new car or wardrobe, a new figure, a vacation, a job.

You create a treasure map by cutting out photographs, words, and phrases from magazines and newspapers and pasting them onto a piece of paper to form a picture that has meaning for you. You can also buy sheets of stick-on letters at an art or stationery store and use them to write words and phrases that have special meaning for you. You can make up anything you like: It's your treasure map, your picture of what you want.

Making a treasure map not only creates a physical picture of what you want, it affords you a period of concentrated thought about your desires while you are creating it. Your mind is totally focused on what you want.

You can make a notebook of treasure maps, a page for each facet of your life. Or you can create your treasure map on a file folder so it will stand up by itself and you can place it where you can see it. A file folder is also easy to fold up and put away when company comes. (One school of thought maintains that you shouldn't share your treasure map with anybody.)

My friends Lynnie and Cheri, on the other hand, created theirs on huge pieces of posterboard and placed them in their bathrooms. It was amazing to me to look at their treasure maps and watch their lives unfold the way they had pictured them. It's not necessary to share your treasure map with anyone, but you can if you want to. Place your treasure map in the best place for *you*, a place where you can see it easily. It's important to look at and affirm your treasure map at least once a day.

Make sure you include pictures of yourself, or at least your face, in your treasure map. Since you are working on your body, cut out pictures of people whose bodies you'd like yours to resemble. Choose them in different poses or participating in your favorite activities. Place a picture of your head on as many pictures of the bodies you like as you can. Remember, it's *you* you are creating.

It is also a good idea to include a picture of something that represents a deity or higher power to you. This does not have to be a conventional deity. It can be anything you pray or talk to, anything you believe will help you get what you want. In the movie *Shirley Valentine*, Shirley talked to a wall.

You also want to place a positive affirmation on your treasure map. The one I use is: "This or something better now manifests in my life with good to all concerned." It is important to include "good to all concerned" in all your treasure maps.

I have found in treasure mapping that you get the *essence* of what you want, not *exactly* what you want. If you expect to get an exact duplicate of what you cut out of a magazine, you do not give the universe room to manifest. The pictures we have in our minds are limited by our experience and scenes from the past. The universe has to have room to bring you something new. Even though your treasure map is made up of pictures, these pictures merely represent what you want—they're not the exact image.

You can spend one afternoon or evening creating a treasure map or spread the process out over time, whatever suits you. Recently I created a treasure map that took three weeks to make, starting with the day I bought the magazines to the day I finished the map. My mind was busy with thoughts of the project off and on for the whole time. I had never spent so much "positive thinking" time on this aspect of my life before. Spending so much time on it only helped the process.

## WHAT YOU WILL NEED:

Magazines and/or newspapers

Scissors

Paste or glue

Letters, the kind that rub off a sheet, obtainable at art stores (optional)

Posterboard, notebook paper, or file folders

A good imagination

Start cutting and pasting today, and have fun.

## DAILY EXERCISES

### Becoming Aware Exercise

Continue to notice how you feel after you eat and write your observations in your food diary.

### What Does Your Body Want?

Ask your body "What do you want to do today?" Now ask your body "What do you want to eat today?" Write down in your journal what you heard, and be sure to give your body what it wants during the day.

Continue the exercise program from Days 5–12 and add the following exercises.

## 13 ▶ **44** ARM REACH PULSE (oblique abdominals)

• • • • • • • • • • • • • • • • • • • • • • • • • • • • • • • • • • • • • • • • • •

Lie on the floor with your knees bent, and, with both hands by your sides or keeping your left hand behind your neck to support your head, lower your right arm to your side. Your feet should be 12 inches apart. Maintain a C curve and lift your shoulders off the floor to shoulder blade height. Holding your upper back off the floor, exhale and reach your right arm toward your right heel. Inhale and return to the original position with your shoulders off the floor and your pelvis tucked. Repeat 8 times. Be sure to say the affirmations for abdominals.

Again, with both hands by your sides or now placing your right hand behind your neck, straighten your left arm to your side. Exhale and reach your left hand toward your left heel. Inhale and return to the original position with your shoulders off the floor and your pelvis tucked. Repeat 8 times, saying the affirmations. Do the whole series one more time.

| AFFIRMATIONS FOR ABDOMINALS |
|---|
| *I have a great stomach. My stomach loves to exercise. It gets stronger and more beautiful every day. I easily understand all sides of a situation and trust my judgment with new ideas. I love my inner knowing and move forward in life safely, knowing my intuition is correct. I know and am safe in my knowing.* |

# 45 OPPOSITE SHOULDER REACH (oblique abdominals)

Lie with your knees bent. Keep your right hand behind your neck and stretch your left hand out, palm down. Raise your shoulders off the floor to shoulder blade level. Keeping your left arm outstretched and right elbow open, exhale and raise your right shoulder toward your left knee to the count of 2. Inhale and lower your shoulder almost to the floor to the count of 2. Repeat 12 times, saying the affirmations for abdominals in Exercise 44.

Place your left hand behind your neck and stretch your right arm out to the side. Keeping your shoulders off the floor, exhale and raise your left shoulder toward your right knee to the count of 2. Inhale and lower your shoulder almost to the floor to the count of 2. Repeat 12 times. Do the entire series once more as you say the affirmations for abdominals.

# 46 ROTATION CRUNCH (oblique abdominals)

Lie with your knees bent. Place your left ankle on your right thigh close to your knee. Raise your shoulders slightly off the floor to shoulder blade level.

Exhale and raise your upper body up toward your knees to the count of 1. Continue to exhale and rotate your torso left, lifting your right shoulder further toward your left knee to the count of 2. Inhale and turn your torso straight again to the count of 1; continue to inhale and lower your torso almost to the floor to the count of 2. Repeat 12 times, saying the affirmations for abdominals in Exercise 44. Repeat with your right ankle on your left thigh 12 times as you say the affirmations. Do the entire series once more.

13

## Mind Chatter Turnarounds

In your journal, write down all the negative things your mind told you while you were exercising and turn them around.

## Affirmation Exercise

Create an affirmation for today as described on pages 70–71. Write it down in your journal and be sure to refer to it during the day.

## Visualization Exercise

Create a visualization for your affirmation as described on pages 107–108.

## What Is Your Body Saying Today?

Ask your body what it wants to say to you today. Write down the areas you are having problems with and interpret what they mean to you. Look up the affirmations in Appendix A and select one for today, or create one that works for you.

## Today's Nurture

Look over your nurtures list on page 115, add more if you've thought of more, and choose one. Make sure you give it to yourself by the end of the day.

## Telling the Truth Exercise

List three opportunities you had for telling the truth today. Did you tell it? If not, examine what stood in your way. If you did tell it . . . celebrate!

## Character Dialogue

What did your character say to you today? What does it need? What does it want? How do you feel about your character today? Write your observations in your journal.

*Make an appointment with yourself for tomorrow:*

Name: _____

Date: _____

Book time: _____

Exercise time: _____

## EVENING PROCESS

Review your goals.

Review today's tasks.

Check off those you have accomplished.

Look back at the "What Does Your Body Want?" exercise. Did you give it what it wants today? If not, what has to change? Write the answer in your journal.

### Ten End-of-the-Day Acknowledgments

1. _____
2. _____
3. _____
4. _____
5. _____
6. _____
7. _____
8. _____
9. _____
10. _____

*Q: How do you eat an elephant?*
*A: One bite at a time.*

## WEEK IN REVIEW

Restate the goal as set for you on Day 1 and your personal goal.

_____

_____

_____

_____

Review and restate today's tasks: _____

_____

_____

_____

_____

Take 10 minutes to review your journal and food diary. What have you learned about the way you talk to yourself? How are you feeling after you eat? Have you noticed which foods make you feel good and which ones make you feel uncomfortable? Are you comfortable with your affirmations? How does it feel to be more aware of your likes and dislikes? How does it feel to exercise? Where do you need to spend more time? What haven't you done? What are you consistently not doing? Remember, it's your program. In order for it to work, you have to work it. Have fun and continue on.

## DAILY EXERCISES

### Becoming Aware Exercise

Continue to notice how you feel after you eat and to write your observations in your food diary.

## What Does Your Body Want?

Ask your body what it wants to do today in the area of exercise. Ask your body what it wants to eat today. Write down your answers in your journal. Be sure you give these things to your body at some time during the day.

## Physical Exercises

Continue the exercise program from Days 5–13 and add the following exercises.

# 47  CRUNCHES (full abdominals)

Lie with your knees bent, feet flat on the floor. Place your hands behind your neck with your elbows out to the side. Raise your chin slightly as if you were holding an orange under it. Be sure your pelvis is tucked in a C curve, and raise your shoulders off the floor slightly. Exhale and pull your torso forward toward your knees to the count of 2. Inhale and lower your torso almost to the floor to the count of 2. Use resistance as you lower your torso and repeat 16 times as you say the affirmations for abdominals.

> **AFFIRMATIONS FOR ABDOMINALS**
>
> *I love my stomach. It is strong and beautiful. My abdominal muscles love to exercise. They are doing a good job and are getting stronger every day. I trust my inner knowing and digest all new ideas easily. It is fun to learn new information. I trust myself and the world I live in. I love my stomach.*

# 48 RAISED-LEG CRUNCHES (full abdominals)

Lie with your knees bent. Raise your legs straight up, perpendicular to the floor, and cross your ankles. Keeping your hands behind your neck, your pelvis tucked in a C curve, and your shoulders slightly raised off the floor, pulse (lift) your upper body toward your feet. Inhale and lower your torso almost to the floor. Repeat 16 times and say the affirmations for abdominals in Exercise 47.

# 49 ONE-LEG STRETCH (full abdominals)

Lie with your knees bent. Keep your right foot on the floor and stretch your left leg out at a 45-degree angle to the floor. Stretch both arms out in front of you, and bring your body into a curved position. From this curved position pulse your upper body 16 times toward your left foot. Always exhale on the uplift, the exertion.

Relax a moment. Place your left foot on the floor and straighten your right leg out at a 45-degree angle. Keeping your arms stretched out in front of you, raise your body into a curve and pulse 16 times toward your right foot. Rest a moment and repeat the entire exercise. Be sure to say the affirmations for your abdominals in Exercise 47 during the whole exercise.

## Mind Chatter Turnarounds

In your journal, write down all the negative things your mind told you while you were exercising and turn them around.

## Affirmation Exercise

Create an affirmation for today. Write it down in your journal and be sure to refer to it during the day.

## Visualization Exercise

Create a visualization for your affirmation.

## What Is Your Body Saying Today?

Ask your body what it wants to say to you today. Write down the areas you are having problems with and interpret what they mean to you. Create an affirmation for your body.

## Today's Nurture

Look over your nurtures list, add more if you've thought of more, and choose one to give to yourself today.

## Telling the Truth Exercise

Write down three opportunities you had for telling the truth to yourself and others during the day. Write down whether you told the truth successfully. If you didn't, what has to happen to empower you in this area?

## Character Dialogue

What did your character say to you today? Have you noticed any changes in your relationship with your character?

## Treasure Mapping Exercise

Spend time on your treasure map.

*Make an appointment with yourself for tomorrow:*

Name: _____

Date: _____

Book time: _____

Exercise time: _____

## EVENING PROCESS

Review your goal.

Review today's tasks.

Check off those you have accomplished.

Look back at the "What Does Your Body Want?" exercise. Did you give it what it wants today? If not, what has to change? Write the answer in your journal.

## Ten End-of-the-Day Acknowledgments

1. _____

2. _____

3. _____

4. _____

5. _____

6. _____

7. _____

8. _____

9. _____

10. _____

14

## WHAT'S DIFFERENT?

Restate the goal as set for you on Day 1 and your personal goal.

_____

_____

_____

_____

Review and restate today's tasks: _____

_____

_____

_____

_____

_____

In my experience with MetaFitness I have found that when people start working the program, and begin to change their relationship with their body, other things change as well. Friends and acquaintances start telling them how beautiful they are. The friends may attribute the new look to a new hairstyle, sudden weight loss, new clothes—and nothing has changed outwardly at all.

What has changed since you started reading this book is your attitude toward yourself. Maybe I should have warned you at the beginning: Don't be surprised by anything that happens in these 21 days. You're coming into your own power and it's a place you may not be familiar with.

You may find that old friends no longer interest you. This can be a sad time as you let go of them. But if they have been a reflection of your worst thoughts about yourself, they no longer serve you. Don't be afraid. The universe abhors a vacuum and will fill the space immediately. Since you have a new attitude toward yourself, your new friends will reflect that attitude.

As you become more loving toward yourself, you will not allow yourself to be treated badly. This may come as a shock to people who have been used to mistreating you. Let them be shocked. And stand your ground. You may find that a partner who has been difficult to live with in the past suddenly becomes easy. This is because your attitude about yourself has changed, not because of him or her. Conversely, you may find that a veritable pussycat has turned into a tiger. Chances are you have been going out of your way to keep the tiger at bay and now you no longer want to.

You will also find that your relationship to food has changed. It may come as a terrible disappointment to the date who's been taking you to McDonald's for months when he discovers you won't settle for anything other than a salad and a veginut burger.

You will also find that you look different to yourself. This can be an unsettling period, something akin to walking into the mirror room at the funhouse. One day you look fat, one day you look thin; one day you look short, one day you look tall—you're never quite sure at this time who's going to be in the mirror. Eventually you will see yourself with loving eyes, no matter what you look like.

What are some of the changes you have noticed in your life since you began this program?


## Example

I now know it's *my* voice that's telling me awful things and I can choose whether or not to listen to it.

I get lots of compliments.

I'm not as hungry as I used to be.

I feel better about my body.

I laugh more.

I've discovered I like fresh vegetables.

I don't have to eat lima beans.

I'm beginning to enjoy exercise. My body really likes to move.

My boyfriend doesn't tell me I "should lose weight."

It's easier for me to say no.

I'm nicer to myself.

My body is my friend.

Your turn: _____

_____

_____

_____

_____

_____

_____

_____

_____

_____

How do you feel about yourself? _____

_____

_____

## DAILY EXERCISES

### Becoming Aware Exercise

Continue to notice how you feel after you eat and to write your observations in your food diary.

### What Does Your Body Want?

Ask your body what it wants in the way of exercise today. Ask your body how it wants to eat today. Record your answers and give yourself what you want.

### Physical Exercises

Continue the exercise program from Days 5–14 and add the following exercises.

# 50 STRETCH (flexibility)

Lie flat on your back and stretch your arms up over your head. Stretch out as long as you possibly can. Be sure to keep breathing and hold the stretch 10 to 20 seconds as you say the affirmations for flexibility, then release.

## AFFIRMATIONS FOR FLEXIBILITY

*My body is very flexible. It is easy for me to stretch in my life. I love reaching farther than I have ever gone before. It is easy for me to be flexible.*

**15**

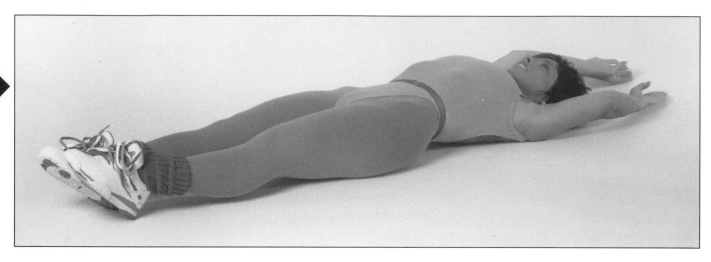

# 51 CHEST LIFT STRETCH (flexibility, chest, and abdominals)

Lie on your stomach, your legs outstretched and feet together. Place your hands by your chest and, leaning on your elbows, gently raise your chest off the floor. Hold 10 to 20 seconds as you say the affirmations for chest and abdominals, then relax. Be sure your back is comfortable during this stretch.

> **AFFIRMATIONS FOR CHEST AND ABDOMINALS**
>
> **Chest:** *I love life. It is easy for me to love and be loved. I have a beautiful, strong, and flexible chest. I love my chest.*
> **Abdominals:** *I have a great stomach. It is firm and beautiful. I am safe trusting my inner knowing and am flexible in all my ideas.*

15

# 52 TORSO TWIST STRETCH (flexibility, back, and midriff)

**15**

*Knees bent:* Lie on your back, knees bent, feet flat on the floor. Tuck your pelvis under in a C curve, and stretch your arms out to either side to form a T. Exhale and slowly lower your bent knees to the right. Your right leg will rest on the floor. Hold this position as you keep both shoulders on or close to the floor and inhale as you look left. Breathe normally and hold 10 to 20 seconds as you repeat the affirmations for back and midriff. Exhale again, slowly raise your knees over your chest, and then lower them to your left. Keeping your shoulders on or close to the floor, inhale as you look to your right. Breathe normally and hold 10 to 20 seconds as you repeat the affirmations.

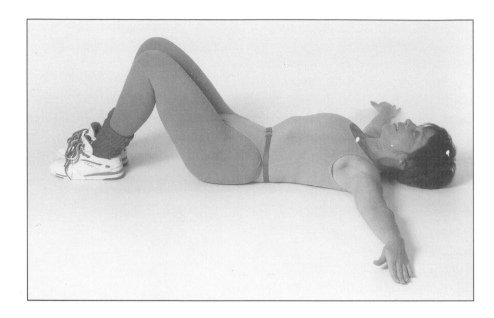

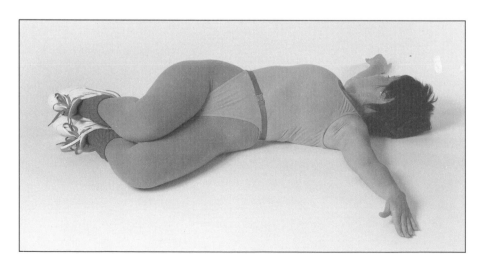

*Leg straight:*  Continue to lie on the floor on your back with your knees bent. Straighten your right leg and lower your bent left leg over it to the right. Keep your shoulders on the floor and look to the left. Hold this position 10 to 20 seconds while you say the affirmations for midriff and back.

Come back to your original position. Bend your right leg and straighten your left. Lower your bent right leg over your left, and turn your head to the right. Hold 10 to 20 seconds as you say the affirmations.

## AFFIRMATIONS FOR BACK AND MIDRIFF

**Back:**  *I love my back. It is strong and flexible. I am supported and have all that I need. I bend easily in any direction.*

**Midriff:**  *I have a beautiful midriff. It is toned, strong, and flexible. It is easy for me to express my emotions. I am safe feeling my emotions. I love my midriff.*

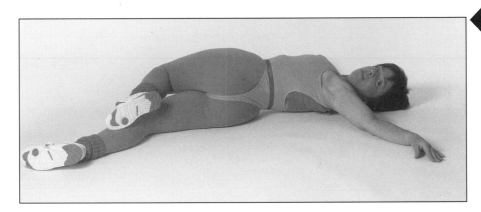

**15**

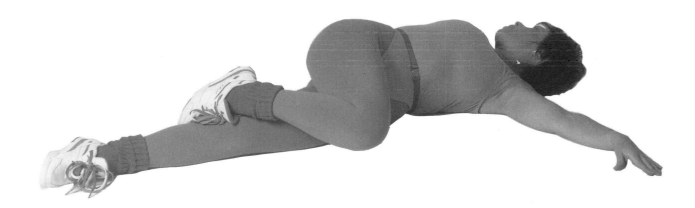

## Mind Chatter Turnarounds

In your journal, write down all the negative things your mind told you while you were exercising and turn them around.

## Affirmation Exercise

Create your affirmation for today.

## Visualization Exercise

Create a visualization for that affirmation.

## What Is Your Body Saying Today?

Ask your body what it wants to say to you. Write down the areas you are having problems with and interpret what they mean to you. Create an affirmation for your body.

## Today's Nurture

Look over your nurtures list, add more if you've thought of more, and choose one to give to yourself today.

## Telling the Truth Exercise

Write down three opportunities you had for telling the truth today. How are you doing in this department?

## Character Dialogue

Write down what your character said to you today.

## Treasure Mapping Exercise

Spend time on your treasure map.

*Make an appointment with yourself for tomorrow:*

Name: _____

Date: _____

Book time: _____

Exercise time: _____

## EVENING PROCESS

Review your goal.
Review today's tasks.

Check off those you have accomplished.

Go back to the "What Does Your Body Want?" exercise.

Did you give it what it wanted? If not, what has to change?

### Ten End-of-the-Day Acknowledgments

1. _____

2. _____

3. _____

4. _____

5. _____

6. _____

7. _____

8. _____

9. _____

10. _____

**15**

## YOU HAVE THE POWER

Review and restate your goals and tasks.

Have you ever noticed how a thin person eats? Have you ever noticed how a person who is truly comfortable with his or her body exercises? Thin people usually leave food on their plates; if they don't want something, they don't eat it. If they want something that's very rich, they usually eat only part of it. Thin people eat only when they are hungry. They never eat in anticipation of being hungry. They stop when they're full. They listen to their body.

Fit people exercise according to the way they feel. Fit people love to move. They do things they like to do. They exercise on a fairly regular schedule. If they don't feel well, they don't exercise. If they hurt, they stop.

You can eat and exercise the way thin and fit people do. It's all about becoming aware, changing your habits, and doing what you like to do.

Make a list of how you normally eat.

**Example**

I eat when it's time to eat, whether I'm hungry or not.

I finish everything on my plate.

I rarely have dessert.

I can't stop snacking.

Your turn: _____

_____

_____

_____

_____

Now make a list of how you would like to eat.

**Example**

I would like to only eat when I'm hungry.

I want to be able to leave food on my plate.

I want to be able to order dessert and eat only a little bit of it.

Your turn: _____

_____

_____

_____

_____

Now make a list of how you normally exercise.

**Example**

I don't.

I wait until I'm too tired and then I feel awful.

I push myself too hard, make myself hurt, go for the burn.

I exercise just right.

Your turn: _____

_____

_____

_____

_____

Make a list of how you would like to exercise.

**Example**

I want to exercise every morning for half an hour.

I want to go dancing at least once a week.

I want to be able to exercise without feeling I have to push myself.

Your turn: _____

_____

_____

_____

Take a moment and look over your lists. Decide how you're going to eat and exercise today. Write it down. But the schedule you are creating for yourself is not to be made in cement. Think of it as an opportunity to eat and exercise in a certain way and if you miss, it's okay.

## Example

I'm going to eat only when I'm hungry and I'm going to leave food on my plate and decline dessert if I'm satisfied.

I'm going to exercise for half an hour to my favorite music.

I'm not going to exercise today; I feel like resting my body.

Your turn: _____

_____

_____

_____

_____

Create an affirmation out of how you want to eat and exercise today.

## Example

I eat as much as I need to be satisfied and I gladly exercise half an hour. I feel great!

Your turn: _____

_____

Copy your affirmation onto a separate piece of paper and put it where you can see it often during the day.

# DAILY EXERCISES

## Becoming Aware Exercise

Continue to notice how you feel after you eat and write your observations in your food diary.

## What Does Your Body Want?

Ask your body how it wants to exercise today. Ask your body what it wants to eat. Record your answers in your journal. Are you following what your body tells you yet? If not, spend some time with your journal, asking

16

your subconscious mind what stands between you and giving your body what it wants.

## Physical Exercises

Continue your program from Days 5–15 and add the following exercises. For tomorrow's exercises, you will need a pair of two- to five-pound ankle weights.

16

# 53 MODIFIED PUSH-UPS (arms, upper back, chest)

You can do a modified push-up one of two ways, depending on your level of strength. Start where you are comfortable (where you can do it easily) and progress from there.

*Hands and knees squared:* Get on your hands and knees. Place your hands under your shoulders with your fingers facing forward. To protect your lower back, tuck your pelvis under to form a C curve. Keeping your buttocks in the air and your pel-

vis tucked, inhale and lower your chest toward the floor. Exhale and push your chest away from the floor. Repeat 8 times as you say the affirmations for chest, back, and arms.

*Hands and knees angled:* Get on your hands and knees, keeping your back straight so you form a triangle with the floor. Cross your ankles and raise your feet up behind you. Be sure your hands are placed on the floor directly under your shoulders.

Do not sag or arch your back downward or thrust it upward.

Keeping your body straight, inhale and lower your chest to the floor. Exhale and return to the original position. Repeat 8 times as you say the affirmations for chest, back, and arms.

Repeat the push-up repetitions twice. Be sure to do the stretch exercise, 35, from Day 10, repeated on page 188, between each set of repetitions.

## AFFIRMATIONS FOR CHEST, BACK, AND ARMS

**Chest:** *I love my chest. I am safe giving and receiving love. My life is full of joy and wonder. I love my life. My chest is beautiful, strong, shapely, and well defined.*

**Back:** *My back is beautiful, strong, shapely, and well defined. I am fully supported by life and know all my needs and desires are met in present time. I am safe in the world.*

**Arms:** *My arms are beautiful, strong, supple, and lovely to look at. I embrace my life with joy and handle my life's experiences with ease. I am safe in new experiences and know that all is well in my life.*

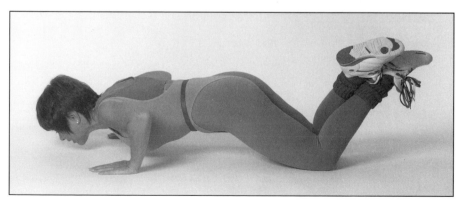

**16**

# 35R SHOULDER/UPPER BACK STRETCH (shoulders and upper back)

◆ ◆ ◆ ◆ ◆ ◆ ◆ ◆ ◆ ◆ ◆ ◆ ◆ ◆ ◆ ◆ ◆ ◆ ◆ ◆ ◆ ◆ ◆ ◆ ◆ ◆ ◆ ◆ ◆ ◆ ◆ ◆ ◆ ◆ ◆ ◆ ◆ ◆ ◆ ◆ ◆ ◆ ◆ ◆

(You may sit for this exercise.) Stand with your feet hip width apart, shoulders relaxed. Tighten your buttocks and abdominals, and tuck your buttocks under in a slight C curve.

Take your right arm and cross it in front of your chest. Place your left hand on your upper right arm and, keeping your shoulders relaxed and lowered, press your right arm close to your chest, stretching the shoulder and upper back muscles. Hold 10 to 20 seconds while you say the shoulder and upper back affirmations, and release.

Change sides and do the same with your left arm.

**16**

### AFFIRMATIONS FOR SHOULDERS AND UPPER BACK

**Shoulders:** *My shoulders are perfect, strong, straight, and very beautiful. I love my life and carry my responsibilities lightly. I follow through easily on all that I do. Life is fun.*

**Upper back:** *My back is beautiful, strong, straight, and lovely to look at. It supports me in my life. I am supported and safe in all that I do. All my needs and desires are met in present time.*

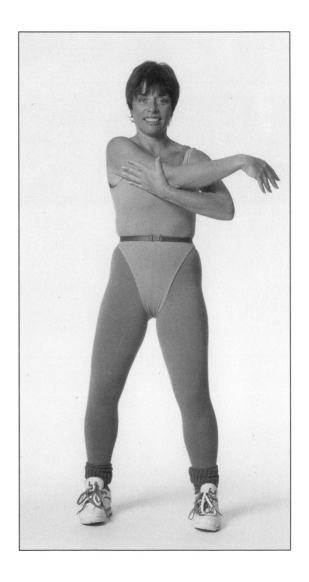

# 54 TRICEP SIT (arms)

You can do the tricep sit one of two ways, depending on your level of strength. Start where you are comfortable (where you can do it easily) and progress from there.

*Sitting:*   Sit on the floor with your legs bent, feet flat on the floor, and your hands resting on the floor behind you. Your fingers should face your body. Tighten your buttocks and abdominals. Inhale and bend your elbows, lowering your body slightly backward. Exhale and return to the upright position. Repeat 8 times while you say the affirmations for arms.

## AFFIRMATIONS FOR ARMS

*My arms are beautiful, strong, supple, and lovely to look at. I embrace my life with joy and handle my life's experiences with ease. I am safe in new experiences and know that all is well in my life.*

*Hands and feet:*   Raise up on your hands and feet with your stomach facing the ceiling. Tighten your buttocks and abdominals. Inhale and bend your elbows, lowering your buttocks and upper body toward the floor. Be sure that you don't just raise and lower your buttocks with-out bending your elbows. Now exhale and straighten your arms, lifting your body upward. Repeat 8 times as you say the affirmations for arms. Repeat the tricep sit one more time. Be sure to do the following stretch exercise, 36, from Day 10.

16

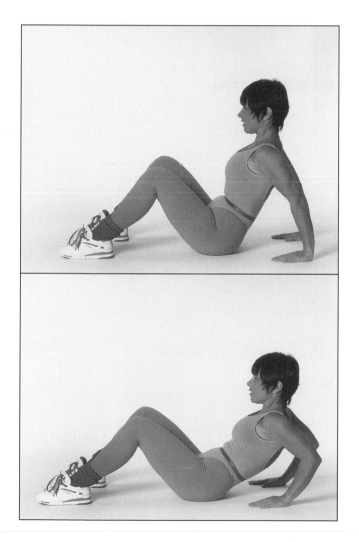

# 36R TRICEP STRETCH (arms)

(You may sit for this exercise.) Stand with your feet hip width apart, shoulders relaxed. Tighten your buttocks and abdominals and tuck your buttocks under in a slight C curve. Raise your right arm straight up, bend it, and place your right hand between your shoulder blades. Take your left hand and place it on your right arm near your elbow. Gently

pull your right arm back behind your head as far as possible. Hold 10 to 20 seconds while you say the affirmations for arms in Exercise 54 and release. Change arms and repeat 10 to 20 seconds.

## Mind Chatter Turnarounds

In your journal, write down all the negative things your mind told you while you were exercising and turn them around.

## Affirmation Exercise

Create an affirmation for today.

## Visualization Exercise

Create a visualization for that affirmation.

## What Is Your Body Saying Today?

Ask your body what it wants to say to you. Write down the areas you are having problems with and interpret what they mean to you. Create an affirmation to turn the problem around.

## Today's Nurture

Look over your nurtures list. Choose one and give it to yourself by the end of the day.

## Telling the Truth Exercise

Write down three opportunities you had to tell yourself and others the truth today. Write down any truth-telling anecdotes you find interesting.

## Character Dialogue

What did your character say to you today? Are you noticing any changes (for example, has George appeared)?

## Noticing Changes Exercise

Write down any changes you notice, anywhere in your life.

## Treasure Mapping Exercise

Spend time on your treasure map.

*Make an appointment with yourself for tomorrow:*

Name: _____

Date: _____

Book time: _____

Exercise time: _____

## EVENING PROCESS

Review your goal.

Review today's tasks.

Check off those you have accomplished.

Look back at the "What Does Your Body Want?" exercise. Did you give it what it wants today? If not, what has to change? Write the answer in your journal.

## Ten End-of-the-Day Acknowledgments

1. _____

2. _____

3. _____

4. _____

5. _____

6. _____

7. _____

8. _____

9. _____

10. _____

16

*The constant assertion of belief is an indication of fear.*

J. Krishnamurti

## CHANGING BELIEFS

Review and restate your goals and tasks.
  Write tasks for Days 18–21.

Day 18: _____

_____

Day 19: _____

_____

Day 20: _____

_____

Day 21: _____

_____

Have you noticed any changes in your beliefs about yourself or your life? In three parallel columns, list your old beliefs about eating, your newly developing beliefs about eating, and the beliefs you would like to adopt.

### Example

| Old beliefs | Emerging beliefs | What I want to believe |
|---|---|---|
| I believed I had to finish everything on my plate. | I believe I can leave food on my plate most of the time. | I can leave food on my plate any time I want to. |
| I believed I had to eat what was given to me. | I can refuse what I don't want most of the time. | I can say no whenever I choose. |

Your turn:

| Old beliefs | Emerging beliefs | What I want to believe |
| --- | --- | --- |
| _____ | _____ | _____ |
| _____ | _____ | _____ |
| _____ | _____ | _____ |
| _____ | _____ | _____ |
| _____ | _____ | _____ |
| _____ | _____ | _____ |
| _____ | _____ | _____ |
| _____ | _____ | _____ |
| _____ | _____ | _____ |
| _____ | _____ | _____ |
| _____ | _____ | _____ |

In three parallel columns, list your old beliefs about exercise, your newly developing beliefs about exercise, and what you want to believe about exercise.

| Old beliefs | Emerging beliefs | What I want to believe |
| --- | --- | --- |
| _____ | _____ | _____ |
| _____ | _____ | _____ |
| _____ | _____ | _____ |
| _____ | _____ | _____ |
| _____ | _____ | _____ |
| _____ | _____ | _____ |
| _____ | _____ | _____ |
| _____ | _____ | _____ |
| _____ | _____ | _____ |
| _____ | _____ | _____ |
| _____ | _____ | _____ |
| _____ | _____ | _____ |

In three parallel columns, list your old beliefs about your body, your newly developing beliefs about your body, and what you want to believe about your body.

| Old beliefs | Emerging beliefs | What I want to believe |
| --- | --- | --- |
| _____ | _____ | _____ |
| _____ | _____ | _____ |
| _____ | _____ | _____ |
| _____ | _____ | _____ |
| _____ | _____ | _____ |
| _____ | _____ | _____ |
| _____ | _____ | _____ |
| _____ | _____ | _____ |
| _____ | _____ | _____ |
| _____ | _____ | _____ |
| _____ | _____ | _____ |
| _____ | _____ | _____ |

## DAILY EXERCISES

### Becoming Aware Exercise

Continue to notice how you feel after you eat. Write your observations in your food diary.

### What Does Your Body Want?

Ask your body how it wants to exercise today. Ask your body what it wants to eat. Record your answers in your journal.

### Physical Exercises

Continue the program from Days 5–16 and add the following exercises.

*Note:* Do all three exercises on one side before turning over to repeat with the other leg. Strap a 2- to 5-pound ankle weight onto each ankle for these exercises.

# 55 LEG LIFTS (thighs)

Lie on your left side. Bend both knees to form a 45-degree angle. Prop your head on your left hand. Tuck your buttocks under in a slight C curve. Place your right hand on the floor in front of you for balance. Raise your bent right leg slightly and hold it in this position. This is your starting position.

Exhale and raise your bent right leg higher. Be sure your foot is level with or slightly higher than your knee. Inhale and lower your right leg almost to touch the left leg, your starting position. Continue in this manner, never touching your left leg with your right, 16 times and then rest a moment. Repeat the affirmations for legs as you do this exercise.

**17**

| AFFIRMATIONS FOR LEGS |
| :---: |

*I love my legs. They are beautiful, strong, flexible, well defined, and lovely to look at. They carry me through life with joy. I move forward with grace and ease. I am willing to move forward into my future knowing I am safe and all is well in my life. My future holds joy and I am at peace with myself as I move into it.*

# 56 LEG KICKS (thighs)

• • • • • • • • • • • • • • • • • • • • • • • • • • • • • • • • • • • • • • • • • • • • • • • •

Continue to lie as before. Your legs should remain bent at a 45-degree angle. Slowly bring your right knee up toward your chest. Exhale and straighten your right leg straight out and down to form a straight line with your body. Inhale and bend, exhale and straighten, never touching your left leg with your right. Repeat 16 times as you say the affirmations for legs in Exercise 55 and then rest a moment.

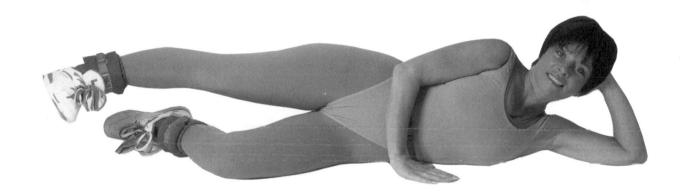

# 57 STRAIGHT LEG LIFTS (thighs)

Continue to lie as before, head resting on your left hand, knees bent with your legs forming a 45-degree angle. Straighten your right leg out and flex your foot so that your heel presses away from your body and your toes are pulled toward your face. Raise your straight right leg slightly and turn your toes inward (your heel is now higher than your toes). Keeping your legs straight, with your knees soft and your foot flexed, exhale and raise your right leg. Inhale and lower almost to your left leg. Exhale and raise, inhale and lower, never touching your left leg with your right. Repeat 16 times as you say the affirmations for legs in Exercise 55.

Turn over and repeat Exercises 55–57 on your right side as you continue saying the affirmations for legs.

**17**

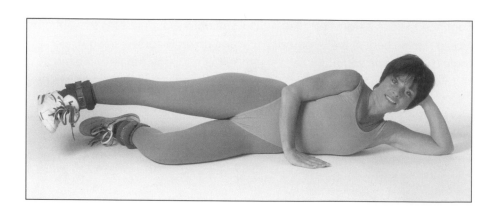

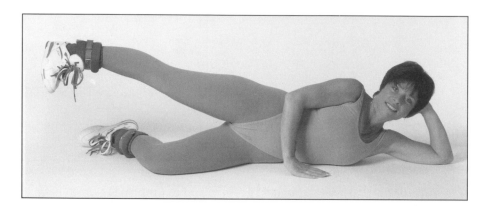

## Mind Chatter Turnarounds

In your journal, write down all the negative things your mind told you while you were exercising and turn them around.

## Affirmation Exercise

Create an affirmation for today.

## Visualization Exercise

Create a visualization for that affirmation.

## What Is Your Body Saying Today?

Ask your body how it feels today. Write down the areas of stress and interpret what they mean to you. Create an affirmation for the problem.

## Today's Nurture

Look over your nurtures list. Choose one to give to yourself.

## Telling the Truth Exercise

How many opportunities have you had to tell the truth to yourself and others today? Did you take advantage of those opportunities? Did you acknowledge and celebrate the fact that you told the truth? If you didn't yet, do so now.

## Character Dialogue

What does your character have to say to you today? Have you noticed any changes in your relationship with your character? Have any side characters appeared?

## Noticing Changes Exercise

Have you noticed any changes in yourself, your life, or the people around you? Write them down in your journal.

## Empowerment Exercise

Have you noticed an area where you are surrendering your power to food, old habits, or other people? What has to happen to empower you to make a different choice and empower yourself?

## Treasure Mapping Exercise

Spend time on your treasure map.

*Make your appointment with yourself for tomorrow:*

Name: _____

Date: _____

Book time: _____

Exercise time: _____

## EVENING PROCESS

Review your goal.

Review today's tasks.

Check off those you have accomplished.

Look back at the "What Does Your Body Want?" exercise. Did you give it what it wants today? If not, what has to change? Write the answer in your journal.

## Ten End-of-the-Day Acknowledgments

1. _____

2. _____

3. _____

4. _____

5. _____

6. _____

7. _____

8. _____

9. _____

10. _____

**17**

We *live in a fantasy world, a
world of illusion. The great
task in life is to find reality.*

Iris Murdoch

## THE MIRROR GAME

Review and restate your goals and tasks.

If you want to know what's going on inside you, take a look at what's going on outside you. Every person you notice reflects an aspect of yourself. Every situation that you consciously experience mirrors a belief or thought you have had inside.

### Example

Sheila has an original, creative mind. She spends a lot of time in her imagination devising new ideas and artistic concepts, and synthesizing apparently unrelated concepts into something new. But she has always had difficulty memorizing, learning arithmetic, spelling, and logical skills. Because of the way she thinks, she did not do particularly well in school, which is set up to reward rote regurgitation at the expense of creative thought. Because she was not consistently an A student, she believed she was stupid. It was not until she was in her 40s that she discovered her intelligence, and it was through the mirror game that she made the discovery.

When Sheila came to me, she was overweight and self-effacing; she was very tough on herself. During one of our sessions I asked her about her friends. She said, "Oh, they're nothing like me. They're all very smart, very beautiful, and lots of fun. I'm none of those things. I may be fun, but I'm not at all smart, and I'm much too fat."

I replied, "Then why do they bother to hang out with you? Do they feel sorry for you?"

She looked at me quizzically. "What do you mean?"

"Well, why would smart people hang out with a dumb person? What would be in it for them? They might have a co-worker who's not so smart, but a friend?"

"You mean I'm smart?"

"Well, think about it."

Sheila thought about it, and the fine bones of her beautiful face lit up as she began to laugh. "You mean I'm thin, too?"

"No, not thin, just beautiful."

It took Sheila a while to integrate this new information, but as she worked with it she began to operate as a beautiful and intelligent person. She stopped letting her false beliefs limit her and began to thoroughly enjoy the people around her as an equal among peers.

It is not possible to see yourself in your entirety. That's why there are other people in your life. They reflect aspects of yourself you cannot always or are unwilling to see. You will like some of these aspects and some of them you may not like. The friends you want to be like as well as the friends who make you uncomfortable are all reflected parts of yourself. They are an opportunity for you to see your own multifaceted personality. What's important here is not to judge but to notice. The mirror game will give you the opportunity to see the parts of yourself you like and own them. It will also give you the opportunity to see the parts of yourself you don't like and make peace with them.

## EXERCISE

Write down the aspects of your friends that you most admire. Over the next few weeks, focus your attention on how you mirror them.

### Example

My friend Lynnie is beautiful, intelligent, funny, kind, caring, and artistic. She delights me with her social graces and her ability to make all those around her feel welcome.

My friend Cheri is beautiful, intelligent, kind, caring, a good writer, a leader, an innovative thinker, athletic, sexy, and courageous. She challenges me with her intellectual prowess and delights me with her camaraderie.

Your turn: _____

_____

_____

_____

_____

_____

_____

_____

_____

_____

_____

18

When I first started this exercise, I couldn't see anything beyond the fact that these people were my friends. As my self-esteem grew and I got stronger, I began to see myself as others saw me—which is how I saw my friends.

So the second part of this exercise is to write what you see in yourself that is a reflection of what you see in your friends.

## Example

I am beautiful, intelligent, caring, funny, athletic, sexy, a good writer, a leader, an innovative thinker, kind, and artistic. I also have excellent social graces and intellectual prowess. I make people feel welcome, and I am a good friend.

Your turn: _____

_____

_____

_____

_____

_____

_____

_____

_____

_____

If this exercise is difficult, come back to it again and again. You will begin to see yourself.

The exercise that you have just done is a judgment exercise—*positive* judgment exercise. People usually think of judgment as negative.

When you judge people negatively you look at them and deny that any aspect of their behavior could possibly have anything to do with you. But that is not so. Just as the people you admire mirror aspects of your hidden self, so do people you don't like. I find that the qualities I dislike in other people are qualities I am most afraid of in myself.

We are both sides of every coin. We are successes and we are failures, we are good enough and we are not good enough, we are happy and we are sad. When we disown any part of ourselves because we don't like it, it doesn't go away, it just goes underground.

## EXERCISE

Write down the aspects of the people in your life you dislike the most. Over the next few weeks, focus your attention on how you mirror them.

**18**

## Example

My acquaintance, who shall remain nameless, is angry, gauche, loud, condescending, and invasive. When he makes up his mind about someone, he never changes it, even in the face of evidence to the contrary.

Another acquaintance, who shall also remain nameless, is always late, judgmental, thoughtless, and contacts me only when she wants something.

Your turn: _____

_____

_____

_____

_____

_____

_____

_____

_____

This is the hard part. Now, don't go away, don't throw the book across the room, don't quit now that you're on Day 18. How do these people reflect you? It's time to notice the other side of yourself. This is not an exercise in negative judgment, it is an exercise in noticing. Remember, what you resist persists, and once you make peace with all sides of yourself you will create more of what you want in your life.

The second half of this exercise is to write what you see in yourself that is a reflection of people you don't like.

## Example

I hate to admit it, but from time to time I have been angry, gauche, loud, definitely condescending, invasive, judgmental, late, occasionally thoughtless, and I have been known to contact people only when I wanted something from them.

Your turn: _____

_____

_____

_____

_____

_____

18

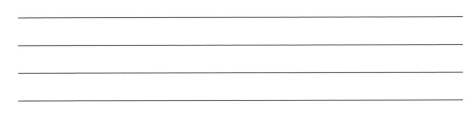

I could make myself wrong for these things, or I can simply notice that they are a part of me. I am both sides of myself, as are you.

## DAILY EXERCISES

### Becoming Aware Exercise

Continue to notice how you feel after you eat and write your observations in your food diary.

### What Does Your Body Want?

Ask your body how it wants to exercise today. Ask your body what it wants to eat. Record your answers in your journal.

### Physical Exercises

Continue the program from Days 5–17 and add the following exercises.

*Note:* Do all three exercises on one side before turning over to repeat with the other leg. Strap a 2- to 5-pound ankle weight onto each ankle for the exercises.

**18**

Lie on your left side. Keep your left leg stretched straight down and place your right foot on the floor out in front of you. Your right leg should be as straight as possible. Prop your head on your left hand and tuck your buttocks under in a slight C curve. Place your right hand on the floor in front of you for balance.

Exhale and lift your straight left leg up off the floor as high as you can. Inhale and lower it almost to the floor. Continue lifting and lowering 16 times as you say the affirmations for legs.

### AFFIRMATIONS FOR LEGS

*I have beautiful legs. They are strong, toned, and well defined. I feel great when I walk and know my legs are perfect and lovely to look at. I release old hurts and welcome my future with grace and ease. I let go of my anger and go forward in my life lighter, happier, and full of joy. Life is a great journey and I've got great legs to carry me forward as I travel onward.*

18

# 59 INNER THIGH CIRCLE (inner thigh)

Continue to lie as in Exercise 58. Holding your left leg up off the floor, exhale and circle your straight left leg forward 4 times. Inhale and circle it back 4 times. Repeat forward and backward circle series 4 times as you say the affirmations for legs in Exercise 58.

18

# 60 HEEL-TO-KNEE LIFT (inner thigh)

Continue to lie as before. This time bend your right leg and place your right foot on the floor behind your straight left leg. Your knee should be upright if possible. Keep your spine in a slight C curve and your buttocks and abdominals tight. Exhale and bend your left knee as you raise your left foot up to touch your right knee. Inhale and return to your original position. Repeat 16 times as you say the affirmations for legs in Exercise 58.

Turn over and repeat Exercises 58–60 on your right side as you continue saying the affirmations for legs.

## Mind Chatter Turnarounds

In your journal, write down all the negative things your mind told you while you were exercising and turn them around.

## Affirmation Exercise

Create an affirmation for today.

## Visualization Exercise

Create a visualization for that affirmation.

## What Is Your Body Saying Today?

Ask your body how it feels today. Write down the areas that are uncomfortable, interpret what they mean, and create an affirmation to turn the feeling around.

## Today's Nurture

Look over your nurtures list. Choose one to give to yourself.

## Telling the Truth Exercise

Review your opportunities for telling the truth today. How are you doing?

## Character Dialogue

What did your character have to say to you today?

## Noticing Changes Exercise

Have you noticed any changes in yourself, your life, or the people around you?

## Empowerment Exercise

Have you noticed where you gave away your power to food, friends, old habits?

## Treasure Mapping Exercise

Spend time on your treasure map.

*Make an appointment with yourself for tomorrow:*

Name: _____

Date: _____

Book time: _____

Exercise time: _____

## EVENING PROCESS

Review your goal.

Review today's tasks.

Check off those you have accomplished.

Look back at the "What Does Your Body Want?" exercise. Did you give it what it wants today? If not, what has to change? Write the answer in your journal.

### Ten End-of-the-Day Acknowledgments

1. _____

2. _____

3. _____

4. _____

5. _____

6. _____

7. _____

8. _____

9. _____

10. _____

DAY 19

## THE MIRROR GAME CONTINUED

Review and restate your goals and tasks.

To continue yesterday's thoughts concerning how you view other people: The subconscious mind does not comprehend "you," "he," "she," "it," or "they." The subconscious mind hears only "I." Whenever you criticize, compliment, or judge another person, your subconscious hears it as a self-criticism, self-compliment, or self-judgment. If you are constantly belittling others and making them wrong, you are making yourself wrong. If you see only faults in other people, your subconscious experiences negative self-judgment. On the other hand, when you see the positive in others, your subconscious experiences positive self-evaluation.

### Write a Letter to a Friend

Write a letter to a friend listing all the wonderful things that you love or like about her or him. You don't have to mail this letter, so don't skimp. When you finish, reread what you wrote, and know that it's all about you.

Your turn: _____

_____

_____

_____

_____

_____

_____

_____

_____

_____

_____

What did you learn about yourself from writing that letter? _____

_____

_____

_____

_____

_____

## DAILY EXERCISES

### Becoming Aware Exercise

Continue to notice how you feel after you eat and record what you notice in your food diary.

### What Does Your Body Want?

Ask your body how it wants to exercise and what it wants to eat today. Record the answers in your journal.

### Physical Exercises

Continue the program from Days 5–18 and add the following exercises.

Strap a 2- to 5-pound ankle weight onto each ankle for these three exercises.

**19**

# 61 PRONE LEG LIFTS (buttocks)

Lie on your stomach. Rest your head on your folded arms. Keep your legs straight with knees soft. Tighten your buttocks and abdominals and, keeping your hipbones on the floor, exhale and raise your straight left leg. Inhale and lower it almost to the floor. Repeat 16 times. Change legs, repeating 16 times with your right leg, while saying the affirmations for the buttocks.

## AFFIRMATIONS FOR BUTTOCKS

*I love my rear end. My buttocks are beautiful, powerful, and strong. My buttocks are the perfect shape. I look great in jeans. I am safe experiencing my power and the power of others. I am very powerful in a way that is congruent with who I am. I love my power and express it wisely and with compassion. The power of others is fun to experience. It is safe to be with powerful people. It is safe for me to be powerful. I'm okay when I'm not powerful, too.*

Get on your elbows and knees. Tighten your buttocks and abdominals and tuck your buttocks under to form a slight C curve. Keeping your hips even, and maintaining your balance, raise your bent left leg slightly off the floor. From this raised-leg position, exhale and raise your bent leg higher, level with your buttocks. Inhale and lower it to the original raised-leg position. Repeat raising and lowering 16 times. Change legs. Repeat 16 times with your right leg. Say the affirmations for buttocks in Exercise 61.

19

# 63 KNEELING STRAIGHT-LEG LIFTS (buttocks)

Stay on your elbows and knees as in Exercise 62. Tighten your buttocks and abdominals and tuck your buttocks under in a slight C curve. Stretch your left leg straight out behind you. Rest your toes on the floor and soften your knee. Exhale, and raise your straight leg up to buttock height. Inhale and lower it again. Repeat 16 times. Change legs. Repeat 16 times with your right leg, saying the affirmations for buttocks in Exercise 61.

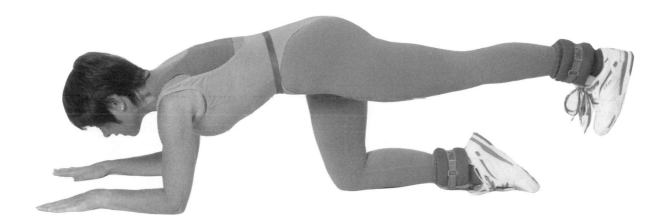

### Mind Chatter Turnarounds

In your journal, write down all the negative things your mind told you while you were exercising and turn them around.

### Affirmation Exercise

Create an affirmation for today.

## Visualization Exercise

Create a visualization for that affirmation.

## What Is Your Body Saying Today?

Ask your body how it feels today. Notice the areas of discomfort, interpret what they mean to you, and create an affirmation to turn them around.

## Today's Nurture

Look over your nurtures list, choose one, and give it to yourself by the end of the day.

## Telling the Truth Exercise

Review your opportunities you had for telling the truth during the day. Are you telling the truth more often or is it still difficult?

## Character Dialogue

What did your character say to you today? How are the two of you doing?

## Noticing Changes Exercise

Notice any changes in your life, yourself, the people around you.

## Empowerment Exercise

Notice any areas where you still give your power over food and your body to old habits, your job, your time schedule, old friends, family, and others.

## Mirror Game

In your journal, write down the things you notice about other people. Be sure to write down both the positive and the negative judgments. Whether you like them or not, what you see in other people are qualities you possess.

## Treasure Mapping Exercise

Spend time on your treasure map.

*Make an appointment with yourself for tomorrow:*

Name: _____

Date: _____

Book time: _____

Exercise time: _____

## EVENING PROCESS

Review your goal.

Review today's tasks.

Check off those you have accomplished.

Look back at the "What Does Your Body Want?" exercise. Did you give it what it wants today? If not, what has to change? Write the answer in your journal.

### Ten End-of-the-Day Acknowledgments

1. _____

2. _____

3. _____

4. _____

5. _____

6. _____

7. _____

8. _____

9. _____

10. _____

**19**

## REFRAMING

Review and restate your goals and tasks.

There is more to this 21-Day Program than simply changing your body. You can change your life, too. As you have learned, your thoughts create your reality. Your thoughts have created the way you are living right now: your lifestyle, your relationships, your home, your work. In your life, as in your body, what you focus on expands. If you continuously complain about your relationships, your financial state, your home, or your work, you will perpetuate everything you are complaining about. If you want things to change, you have to experience them in a positive way. But first you have to notice what you are complaining about.

Many people complain as a manner of conversation. Ever notice how easy it is to get sucked into a conversation about your illnesses, or your weight, or how things are going wrong in the office? Or it's too hot, too cold, too wet, too dry, too too . . . It seems to be easier to focus on the negative than the positive. Unfortunately, focusing on the negative makes you feel bad.

This book and all the exercises in it are about your body, but also about your life. Every body-related exercise can be reframed to apply to life situations as well.

### EXERCISE

Make a list describing some of the complaints about your life you have right now.

### Example

Yesterday Joan and I went to the opera. It was raining. The bus didn't come. We finally took a cab. There was a parade on Fifth Avenue, so we couldn't cross the Park to Lincoln Center. We were going to miss the opera. We walked. We got soaked. We went to the opera wet.

Your turn: _____

_____

_____

_____

_____

## Reframe

Yesterday Joan and I went to the opera. It was raining. The bus didn't come. We finally took a cab. There was a parade on Fifth Avenue, so we couldn't cross the park to Lincoln Center. We were going to miss the opera. We walked. We got soaked. We laughed, we chattered, we noticed the changing colors of the trees, we jumped puddles. We turned the inconvenience into an opportunity to get our exercise, which we wouldn't have gotten if we had stayed in the cab or taken the bus. Our bodies felt great. We were wet and happy. We loved the opera, and our walk in the rain. We could have gotten mad, but that would have ruined everything, including the opera.

In reframing the experience we saw an opportunity in the inconvenience.

Your turn: _____

_____

_____

_____

_____

# DAILY EXERCISES

## Becoming Aware Exercise

Continue to notice how you feel after you eat and record your observations in your food diary.

## What Does Your Body Want?

Continue to ask your body how it wants to exercise and what it wants to eat, recording your findings and following your body's directions.

## Physical Exercises

Continue the program from Days 5–19 and add the following exercises.

# 64 BUTTOCKS STRETCH (buttocks and flexibility)

Sit back on your heels and stretch your arms out in front of you. Hold this position 10 to 20 seconds and say the affirmations for buttocks and flexibility.

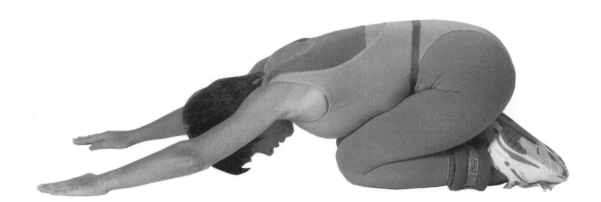

20

# 65 SIDE BUTTOCKS STRETCH (buttocks and flexibility)

Sit up on your heels and rest your hands on the floor in front of you. Exhale and slowly lower your buttocks to the floor on your right. Breathe normally and hold 10 to 20 seconds as you say the affirmations for buttocks and flexibility in Exercise 64. Return to your original kneeling position.

Exhale and slowly lower your buttocks to the floor on your left. Breathe normally and hold 10 to 20 seconds as you say the affirmations.

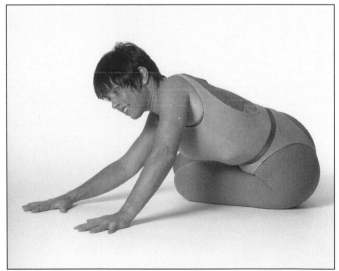

**20**

Sit on the floor. Bend your left knee so that your foot crosses in front of you, and place your right foot over your left thigh. Grasp your right thigh with your left hand. Exhale and twist your torso right, placing your right hand on the floor behind you. Hold your right knee with your arm. Keep breathing normally and hold this position 10 to 20 seconds while you say the affirmations for the back and flexibility.

Change sides and repeat the exercise with your left foot over your right thigh. Hold 10 to 20 seconds and say the affirmations.

## AFFIRMATIONS FOR BACK AND FLEXIBILITY

**Back:** *I love my back. It is strong, beautiful, and very flexible. I am fully supported by life and know that all my needs and desires will be taken care of. I am safe in all areas of my life. It is safe for me to let go of my fears. All is well in my life.*

**Flexibility:** *My body is very flexible. I am flexible in my life as well. It is easy for me to be flexible.*

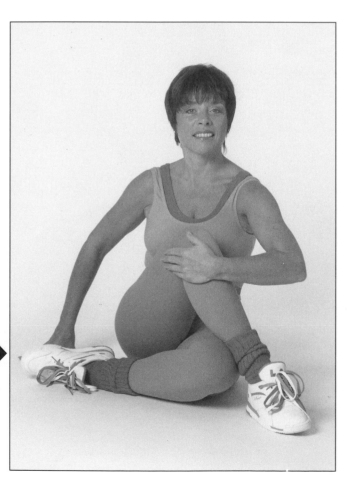

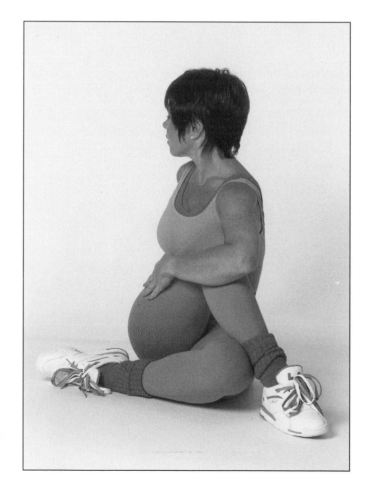

20

## Mind Chatter Turnarounds

In your journal, write down all the negative things your mind told you while you were exercising and turn them around.

## Affirmation Exercise

Create an affirmation for today.

## Visualization Exercise

Create a visualization for that affirmation.

## What Is Your Body Saying Today?

Notice how your body feels today, interpret the aches and pains, and create an affirmation to turn them around.

## Today's Nurture

Look over your nurtures list, choose one, and give it to yourself.

## Telling the Truth Exercise

Notice the opportunities you had for telling the truth today. Have you observed how your body *feels* when you don't tell the truth?

## Character Dialogue

What did your character say to you today?

## Noticing Changes Exercise

Notice how things are changing in your life.

## Empowerment Exercise

Notice areas in your relationships to food, exercise, other people, and your life where you are becoming more powerful.

## Mirror Game

Write down the positive and negative things you noticed in other people today.

## Write a Letter to a Friend Exercise

Write a letter to a friend, listing all the wonderful things you like about her or him.

## Treasure Mapping Exercise

Spend time on your treasure map.

*Make an appointment with yourself for tomorrow:*

Name: _____

Date: _____

Book time: _____

Exercise time: _____

## EVENING PROCESS

Review your goal.

Review today's tasks.

Check off those you have accomplished.

### Ten End-of-the-Day Acknowledgments

1. _____
2. _____
3. _____
4. _____
5. _____
6. _____
7. _____
8. _____
9. _____
10. _____

**20**

## CHANGING BELIEFS

Review and restate your goals and tasks.

On Day 17 you listed your old beliefs about eating, your newly developing beliefs about eating, and the beliefs you would like to adopt. Over the past several days, you have probably made even more changes. In two parallel columns, list your old beliefs about eating and the new beliefs that you have adopted.

**Example**

| *Old beliefs* | *New beliefs* |
| --- | --- |
| I believed I had to finish everything on my plate. | I can, and do, leave food on my plate. |
| I believed I always had to accept what was given to me. | I can, and do, say no if I don't want something and I now know whether I want something or not. |

Your turn:

| *Old beliefs* | *New beliefs* |
| --- | --- |
| _____ | _____ |
| _____ | _____ |
| _____ | _____ |
| _____ | _____ |
| _____ | _____ |

Isn't it amazing what has changed? And all you had to do was change your mind.

## WEEKS IN REVIEW

Take some time right now to look over your journal and review the past 21 days. What have you learned about the way you talk to yourself? How do you feel after you eat? What are the foods you are now choosing to eat? Are you more comfortable with your affirmations? How does it feel to be more aware of likes and dislikes? How does it feel to exercise? Where do you need to spend more time? What haven't you done? What have you consistently avoided doing?

You have come to the end of your 21-Day Program. But it doesn't stop now. What you have learned you will use for the rest of your life. You have begun the process of being good to yourself, of eating well, exercising, and thinking positively. You may forget sometimes, and that's all right. Just notice when you're off track (don't worry—your body will let you know) and get back on. Don't make yourself wrong; it's all part of the process. Don't think that because you've slipped you can never go back to your good habits. One good meal, one exercise session, one positive thought, and you'll be back on track. Now that you've finished, don't forget to continue giving yourself nurtures, and writing down your acknowledgments every night.

## DAILY EXERCISES

### Becoming Aware Exercise

Continue to notice how you feel after you eat. You now have a program for the rest of your life. In the past three weeks you've established consciousness about food. In order to retain control over your food, you have to stay aware. It's as simple as that.

### What Does Your Body Want?

Ask your body how it wants to exercise and what it wants to eat today and give it what it wants. Again, you now have a program for life, a program of working *with* your body to keep you healthy, fit, and trim.

### Physical Exercises

Continue the program from Days 5–20 and add the following exercises.

# 67 HAMSTRING STRETCH (legs and flexibility)

Lie on your back, knees bent, feet flat on the floor. Tighten your buttocks and abdominals and tuck your buttocks under in a slight C curve. Raise your left leg up. Your leg should be straight with your knee soft. Grasp your raised leg with both hands just below the knee. Exhale and pull your leg toward your chest. Inhale and hold it in this position. Exhale again and pull it a little closer to you. Inhale and hold. Breathe normally and hold this position 10 to 20 seconds as you say the affirmations for legs and flexibility. Repeat one more full exhale as you pull your leg even closer. Inhale and hold this position. Breathe normally and say the affirmations as you hold this position 10 to 20 seconds.

## AFFIRMATIONS FOR LEGS AND FLEXIBILITY

**Legs:** *I have beautiful legs. They are strong, toned, and well defined. I feel great when I walk and know my legs are perfect and lovely to look at. I release old hurts and welcome my future with grace and ease. I let go of my anger and go forward in my life lighter, happier, and full of joy. Life is a great journey and I've got great legs to carry me forward as I travel onward.*

**Flexibility:** *I am very flexible in all areas of my life. It is easy for me to be flexible.*

Repeat the entire series with your right leg as you say the affirmations.

21

# 68 BUTTOCKS-HAMSTRING STRETCH (buttocks, legs, and flexibility)

Lie on your back, knees bent, feet flat on the floor. Tighten your buttocks and abdominals and tuck your buttocks under in a slight C curve. Place your left ankle on your right thigh just above the knee, and allow your left knee to turn outward. Exhale and raise your right foot off the floor. Inhale and clasp your right thigh just behind the knee with both hands. Exhale and pull your right thigh toward your torso. Inhale and hold this position. Breathe normally and hold this position 10 to 20 seconds as you say the affirmations for buttocks, legs, and flexibility.

Change legs and do the entire exercise with your left leg while you say the affirmations.

## AFFIRMATIONS FOR BUTTOCKS, LEGS, AND FLEXIBILITY

**Buttocks:** *I love my buttocks. They are strong, toned, and well defined. I am powerful and enjoy the power of others. It is safe for me to be powerful. I express my power with love and compassion.*

**Legs:** *My legs are beautiful, strong, flexible, and very well coordinated. My future is safe. I move into it with grace and ease. I let go of past hurts and upsets, and move forward in my life with joy.*

**Flexibility:** *My body is very flexible. I am flexible in my life as well. It is easy for me to be flexible.*

21

# 69 BACK MASSAGE (back and relaxation)

There are two ways to do the back massage, depending on your level of strength and flexibility. Start where you are comfortable (where you can do it with ease) and progress from there.

*Feet flat:* Lie on your back, knees bent, feet flat on the floor. Tighten your buttocks and abdominals and tuck your buttocks under in a slight C curve. Bend your elbows and place your arms on the floor with your hands by your head. Exhale and lift your tucked buttocks off the floor as high as you can while remaining comfortable. Do not arch your back or lift it beyond the point of comfort. Inhale and slowly lower your buttocks to the floor again, making sure you touch each vertebra to the floor as you go. Your lumbar vertebrae (lower spine) are the last to touch the floor just before your buttocks. Repeat 4 times and say the affirmations for relaxation.

> ## AFFIRMATION FOR RELAXATION
>
> *I am relaxed in my life. All stress and tension are released from my body. I go through life in a relaxed manner, stress- and tension-free. Life is easy; nothing causes me to be stressed. It is easy for me to relax, even in the most extraordinary circumstances. I know I am safe in all areas of my life, and therefore, always feel relaxed and tension-free.*

21

*Plow:* Lie as in the previous exercise. Place your arms by your sides and raise your legs above your torso. Place your feet as close to the floor above your head as you can while remaining comfortable. Your buttocks and lower back should come off the floor. (Do not go up into a shoulder stand; stay on your upper back.) Exhale and slowly lower your legs toward the floor, allowing your back to be massaged by the floor as you lower your legs. You will touch one vertebra to the floor at a time. When your legs are perpendicular to the floor, bend your knees and place your feet on the floor. Repeat the exercise 4 times and say the affirmations for relaxation.

| **AFFIRMATION FOR RELAXATION** |
| :---: |
| *I am relaxed in my life. All stress and tension are released from my body. I go through life in a relaxed manner, stress- and tension-free. Life is easy; nothing causes me to be stressed. It is easy for me to relax, even in the most extraordinary circumstances. I know I am safe in all areas of my life, and therefore, always feel relaxed and tension-free.* |

21

# 70 MORE BACK MASSAGE (relaxation)

Lie on your back, knees bent, feet flat on the floor, hands resting at your sides. Tighten your buttocks and abdominals, and tuck your buttocks under to form a slight C curve. Exhale and slowly raise your buttocks off the floor as you raise your arms over your head to rest above it on the floor. Inhale and hold this position for the count of 4. Exhale, and as you lower your arms, slowly lower your buttocks to the floor again, touching each vertebra to the floor as you lower. Repeat 4 times as you say the affirmation for relaxation in Exercise 69.

21

# 71 TAKE A MOMENT (relaxation)

Lie on your back with your legs stretched out and your arms resting at your sides. Close your eyes. Do nothing. Don't move, don't think, don't say anything to yourself.

Now, after 1 minute of stillness, say to yourself, "I love myself. I am beautiful, smart, courageous, and very special. I'm glad I am who I am and that I have this beautiful body to carry me through life. Yes, I love myself and am glad I'm who I am."

*Congratulations!* You have finished AffirMotions, the exercise program. Do this every day and you will experience the changes in your body and your life that you want.

## Mind Chatter Turnarounds

In your journal, write down all the negative things your mind told you while you were exercising and turn them around. Continue to do this any time you exercise, or indeed, any time you do anything that results in negative mind chatter.

## Affirmation Exercise

Create an affirmation for today.

## Visualization Exercise

Create a visualization for that affirmation.

## What Is Your Body Saying Today?

Ask your body how it feels today. Interpret your aches and pains and create an affirmation to turn them around. Once again, this is a tool to be used regularly. It's important to continue asking your body for the information it's programmed to give you.

## Today's Nurture

Look over your nurtures list, choose one, and give it to yourself. This is a wonderful exercise to continue doing for the rest of your life.

## Telling the Truth Exercise

Notice the opportunities you had for telling the truth today. Remember, continuous truth-telling is one of the most powerful tools for personal growth available to you.

## Character Dialogue

What did your character say to you today?

## Noticing Changes Exercise

Notice how things are changing in your life.

## Empowerment Exercise

Notice whether you are retaining your power with respect to your relationships to food and exercise.

## Mirror Game

Notice things you were aware of in other people today.

## Write a Letter to a Friend Exercise

Keep writing letters to friends, telling them all the wonderful things you love about them.

## Reframing Exercise

Write about something that happened to you that you considered to be an inconvenience. Reframe it into an opportunity.

## Treasure Mapping Exercise

By now you ought to have finished at least one treasure map. Be sure to put it where you can see it every day.

21

## Make an Appointment with Yourself

You have an opportunity to make an appointment with yourself, for yourself, every day. You may want to continue to do this formally. I have found that if I don't rigidly schedule time for myself, I ignore my needs and fall back into old patterns.

### EVENING PROCESS

Review your goal.

Have you achieved the goal you set for yourself 20 days ago?

Take a moment and set new goals for yourself for the next three months.

Review today's tasks.

Check off those you have accomplished.

Set weekly tasks for the next three months.

## Ten End-of-the-Day Acknowledgments

This is another exercise you ought to practice every day.

1. _____
2. _____
3. _____
4. _____
5. _____
6. _____
7. _____
8. _____
9. _____
10. _____

# 6

# The Rest of Your Life

*"Inside an onion is an onion, in an onion, in an onion . . ."*

Joan Meijer-Hirschland
*Organic Gardening* magazine

In the past, I made zillions of New Year's resolutions that faded into the sunset by the end of the month. What was missing from my resolutions was a system for reminding me about them. Goal-setting is your system. Just because you have finished the 21-Day Program doesn't mean you have to stop setting goals.

The body and the mind are very similar to computers: They default to preset values. What that means is that just as a computer will return to its original programming when no new programming is being introduced, your body and mind will return to their most comfortable old habits unless you make it a point to reintroduce your new habits every day. Those old habits are very deep grooves in your subconscious record. Convincing the subconscious mind that you are serious about change takes time and commitment.

Tom Watson, who built IBM from an idea, used to say: "Plan your work—work your plan."

## DESIGN YOUR OWN MAINTENANCE PROGRAM—THAT WORKS FOR YOU

MetaFitness is a long-term commitment to yourself. It is a continuation of those parts of the 21-Day Program that best serve you. Select those awareness exercises—affirmations, visualizations, nurtures, acknowledgment techniques—you want to return to again and again. What feels good to you?

Continue making appointments with yourself. Continue doing what you like. Stay in touch with your body. If you find yourself slipping, recommit and start again. It is important never to make yourself wrong. There will be times when you do slip. In the past, you might have used slipping as an excuse for dropping the program. But not now. Now you get to say, "Oops," and start again. You will be delighted with your results.

One problem with fad diets and exercise programs (but particularly diets) is the concept of beginning and end. First of all, you have to "start the diet." This usually results in several weeks of prediet anticipatory eating. (Sometimes I've eaten for months in anticipation of dieting and *never* gotten to the diet.) For some people, the first three days of any diet are usually hell. Then the mind stops arguing and begins to enjoy what it's doing. The diet always works as long as you stay on it, but many diets say you shouldn't be on them for more than two weeks. What happens when you go off? That's it, you gain back some, if not all or more, of the weight.

I remember living on the grapefruit diet. I would eat exactly what I was told for 10 days. I would lose 7 to 10 pounds. I would go off the diet, as directed, and immediately gain 7 to 10 pounds in 3 days. I would go back on the diet. I maintained my weight for several years this way. Dieting 10 days, overeating 3.

Unlike fad diets, the MetaFitness program is a program for life. You may not lose 10 pounds in 10 days, but neither will you gain 10 pounds in 3. You won't feel as if you can't wait until it's over. You won't dread starting it again. You will find with MetaFitness that you are in charge of what you eat. You eat what your body likes, rather than what others tell you to eat. You eat what your body likes all the time, rather than manipulating food groups for a set period of time. You will never have to *diet* again, because you are always eating consciously. You will never have to turn down an invitation because you are afraid you will overeat.

## DESIGN YOUR OWN DIET

Select what foods your body wants. Spend some time reading Appendix B. Play with different foods. Experiment with what your body likes and doesn't like. Be aware of how you feel. The foods your body likes will make you feel good and keep you in control. The foods it doesn't like will cause discomfort and could result in a binge. Keep asking yourself how you want to feel. I have found that if I'm in a binge cycle, I have only to eat one good meal that completely satisfies my body's nutritional needs to stop it. I have also found that if I'm craving junk foods, I either want to stuff my emotions, or I'm in a binge cycle. All that it takes to stop is the conscious awareness that I'm binging and the decision to stop. Good food does the rest.

## DESIGN YOUR OWN EXERCISE PROGRAM

Everything I've said about diet holds true for exercise. The tombs of New Year's resolutions are littered with the bones of old exercise programs. Again, there is no such thing as a beginning and an end to exercise. Your body is physical; it needs to move.

The MetaFitness program is different from most exercise programs in that it tells you to choose what *you* like to do. Everything that causes your body to move works as long as you do it. The operational words are *do it*.

One of the biggest "reasons" that keep people from exercising is that most experts say you have to work out for certain set periods of time. If they don't have that set period, many people don't exercise. Another "reason" that keeps people from exercising is that they are often told to set unreasonable goals and to push themselves hard to realize them. If they don't reach those high goals immediately, many people get disgusted and stop exercising. And finally, one more "reason" that keeps some (smart) people from exercising is that they are told they have to hurt in order to achieve success. They are told not only that there is value in pain, but that they have to experience this pain on a regular basis for the rest of their lives.

I say, exercise when and for as much time as you can on a daily basis. Set an appointment with yourself and keep it. Do the exercises that make you feel good. You ought to feel better after exercise than you did before.

Listen to your body. Choose the exercises you like. This brings me to yet another "reason" some people don't exercise. If you don't like it, you won't do it. Oh, you might do it for a while, but not over the long term. Contrary to many opinions, there is no rule that says one exercise program is definitive for all people. You have to dare to choose what you like, because ultimately, that's the only one you'll follow through on.

Be aware that exercise is all forms of movement. It is aerobics, conditioning, weight training, jogging, walking, swimming, team sports, bowling, ice skating, skiing, horseback riding, gymnastics, ballroom dancing, ballet, jazz, tap, modern dance, rowing, bike riding, and anything else you can think of. You get to choose.

Just as with dieting, if you never get off, you never have to get back on track. If exercise is part of your life because it's something you enjoy, you never want to get off. If you get off, get back on—no big deal.

## KEEP TRACK OF HOW YOU FEEL

In the 21-Day Program you kept a journal to slow your thought processes so that you could see them. It's a good idea to continue journal work, not only to keep track of how you feel but to keep a record of where you have come from. Keeping a journal will help you stay on track.

And now it's time for the rest of your life.

# Body Parts and Affirmations

## BODY AS TEACHER

What is your body telling you?

*Affirmations*

I am willing to allow my body to be my teacher. My body tells me what I need to know about myself and my life.

## BODY PARTS

### FACE

Your face represents what you show the world. It also represents what you hide from yourself and the world. Inner feelings, even the ones you are not conscious of, very often appear on your face. When you have difficulties with parts of your face, you may want to look at what you are hiding or withholding.

*Affirmations*

My beauty increases every time I look at my face. I love my face. My face expresses who I am. It is safe to be me. I love who I am.

### EYES

Your eyes represent what you see in the world, what you see in your life, and your attitude toward the things you see. They represent your willingness to look at all of your life, and your ability to look honestly at yourself, your relationships, home, work, money, and so on. When you have difficulties with vision, try to figure out what you do not want to see.

*Affirmations*

I have beautiful eyes and my vision is perfect. I see everything that I need to see. I love my eyes. I see myself, my eyes, and my body with love and joy. I see the perfection of my life. I see the perfection of the world around me.

## NOSE

Your nose represents self-recognition, how you see yourself in the world and how comfortable you are with that vision; whether or not you want to be noticed or whether you want to be invisible. It also represents your ability to know what you want and to get what you need.

*Affirmations*

My nose is perfect. I love my nose. I love and approve of myself. I recognize my own true worth and my intuitive ability. I am wonderful.

## CHEEKS

Your cheeks represent your feelings of shame and not being good enough. Notice how you feel when you embarrass yourself and what your cheeks do in reaction. Blemishes or scars tell you of your inner feelings of inadequacy, guilt, or shame.

*Affirmations*

I have beautiful cheeks. They are wonderful to look at and to touch. I am good enough. I accept myself exactly as I am. I love myself.

## MOUTH

Your mouth represents taking in new ideas and nourishment. It is the gateway for expression as well as orifice of reception. Pain in the mouth often represents confusion or an inability to make a decision, or to process what you are learning, experiencing, or trying to express.

*Affirmations*

My mouth is beautiful. It is perfect for me and who I am. I nourish myself with love.

## CHIN

Your chin represents power or powerlessness. How you hold your chin, its shape, and its size can tell you about your inner feelings regarding power. Overly sensitive people, for instance, may continually tuck their chin under as if to protect it from what they fear may hit it. Blemishes on the chin may represent an unwillingness to assume full power, or a need to overcome obstacles to achieve full power.

*Affirmations*

I have a strong, beautiful chin. I love my chin. It is safe to be who I am. I celebrate my power and my vulnerability.

## EARS

Your ears represent your capacity and willingness to hear, to take in and assimilate information. They also tell you whether you are comfortable with your surroundings, or what other people or situations in your life are "telling" you. Earaches often represent anger and frustration. Poor hearing may represent unwillingness to take in new information, that you are turned off to those close to you and do not want to hear them.

*Affirmations*

My ears are perfect. I have beautiful ears. Harmony surrounds me. I listen with love to the pleasant and the good. I am a center for love. I hear with love.

## HAIR

Your hair represents your ability to trust life and allow and acknowledge your feelings. Hair also represents being comfortable with your sexuality—your femininity or masculinity—and your sensuality, and whether you are comfortable allowing yourself to feel and fully enjoy your physical body.

## BALDNESS

Baldness represents fear and tension in life. It represents trying to control rather than trusting life's process. It is almost as if you try so hard to hold on and control your life with your mind that you have cut off the circulation to the roots of your hair. (This, of course, is an image, not a statement of fact.)

*Affirmations*

I have beautiful hair. It is the perfect color, thickness, and style. I am perfect just the way I am. I trust myself. I trust life.

## NECK

Your neck represents balance and flexibility. It serves as the conduit for information between the mind and the body. It represents the ability to perceive what surrounds you, what you just left, what you are going through, and where you are going. The neck represents looking at all sides of a situation. Stiff necks mean you may not be looking honestly at your life and/or you may be unwilling to be flexible in dealing with your life situations.

*Affirmations*

My neck is strong and beautiful. It moves easily, and without tension. I am a problem solver. I see all sides of issues easily and find endless ways of doing things. I am safe and peaceful in my life.

## SHOULDERS

Your shoulders represent carrying and supporting. When there is pain in the shoulders you may be feeling burdened by your life. Your shoulders also represent your willingness to know or not to know, and the way you deal with authority. An elevated right shoulder may mean you deal overtly, an elevated left shoulder may mean you deal covertly.

*Affirmations*

My shoulders are strong and beautiful. They are upright and tension-free. My burdens are light; they support my growth. I choose to allow all my experiences to be joyous and loving.

## UPPER ARMS

Your upper arms represent the capacity to embrace everything life has to offer. They represent the joy or discouragement you feel with everything you experience in life. If you experience pain or weight gain in your arms, you may be holding back from experiencing life fully.

*Affirmations*

My upper arms are beautiful, strong, toned, and firm. I lovingly hold and embrace my experiences with ease and joy.

## ELBOWS

Your elbows represent changing directions in life and accepting new experiences. If you feel stiffness in your elbows, you may be uncomfortable with change. Holding on too tightly to the old may manifest in elbow discomfort. Tennis elbow can be a sign of rigidity.

*Affirmations*

My elbows are perfect. They bend and straighten with ease. I flow with new experiences, new directions, and new changes easily.

## LOWER ARMS

Your lower arms represent your ability to balance and hold whatever you carry in life. They also represent your ability to take the time necessary to center yourself while juggling many things at once. You may experience pain or weakness in your lower arms when you feel you do not have the capacity to handle everything.

*Affirmations*

My lower arms are beautiful and strong. I celebrate the experiences in my life. I hold them with joy and ease.

## WRISTS

Your wrists represent your ability to move with ease while handling your life. They also represent how you move in your life: fluidly, rigidly, lightly, with ease, or with difficulty. Your wrists also represent how you accept or reject pleasure in your life.

*Affirmations*

I have beautiful, strong, and flexible wrists. I handle all my experiences with wisdom, with love, and with ease.

## HANDS

Your hands represent the ability to grasp and handle life. They also represent the limitations we put on ourselves, our skillfulness and dexterity at managing things. Pain in the hands means trying to "handle" everything for yourself and others beyond your capacity, without allowing the emotions that you feel to be expressed. Notice how people express things with their hands. When emotions are not expressed or are turned inward, the hands may experience pain or discomfort. When feelings are not expressed, resentment builds in the body. As the hands are tools of expression, arthritis often occurs in the hands of people who feel thwarted or resentful in their lives. How you hold your hands indicates what you are willing to express and how you want others to see you. Fists indicate anger and resentment, a wishy-washy handshake expresses a blasé attitude toward life, pain can mean feelings of unexpressed resentment.

*Affirmations*

I have beautiful, strong, capable hands. I handle all my experiences with love and joy. I hold my life with ease.

## UPPER BACK

Your upper back guards the heart. It represents safety and support, as well as love and trust. Pain in the upper back can often mean fear, either of giving or receiving love or not being able to trust either oneself or someone else, and most important, not trusting the universe (or Higher Power).

A key concept in back problems is willingness to receive. If you have upper back problems, look at your willingness to receive love and support. Look at your willingness to trust. Look at your belief about whether or not love is or can be there for you. Clearing up upper back problems is a major leap in faith.

My upper back is strong and beautiful. I carry joy and move with ease. I love and approve of myself. Life supports me. I am safe loving and safe being loved.

## MID-BACK

Pain in the mid-back represents a fear of betrayal. "Stabbed in the back" is an American idiom representative of that fear. Another such idiom is "Don't turn your back on him."

Pain in your mid-back could also mean you have subconscious feelings of guilt and being stuck in the "gunk" of life. It also represents fear of being hemmed in or taken advantage of. You might want to look at what guilt you are carrying around that you no longer need, or whether you feel stuck in your life, or whether there are persons or responsibilities you are carrying that you no longer need or want to carry.

*Affirmations*

My middle back is strong, toned, flexible, and beautiful. It is smooth and exactly the way I want it to be. I release the past. I am free to move forward with love in my heart. I am safe in the freedom of my life. I am safe with others.

## LOWER BACK

Your lower back represents support. In this culture, support is represented by money and real property. Pain in the lower back occurs when there is a deep subconscious fear that there is not enough. In many cases the fear revolves around money. This is a tricky one. A person may appear to have plenty of money, may even be a millionaire, but the deep-seated fear and the pain are still there.

Lower back problems may mean a lack of trust that there will always be enough in life. Fear and trust cannot exist in the same space.

*Affirmations*

My lower back is perfect, strong, and flexible. My lower back moves and holds me in comfort and ease. I trust life and am supported by life. I always have everything I need. I am safe.

## CHEST

Your chest represents your ability to take in both love and life. It represents your ability to feel safe in love. The chest houses both the lungs and the heart, two major life centers. Without the lungs to take in oxygen or the heart to pump blood through your body, your body dies. Pain in the chest, depending on where it is located, can be associated with fear, guilt, anger, repression, rigidity, and grief.

The chest is also the center of giving. It is the site where children are nurtured by their mothers. When people comfort or love each other, they clasp each other to their chest. When the ability to give or receive is blocked, pain in the chest (heart or lungs) may follow.

*Affirmations*

My chest is beautiful, well-defined, strong, and powerful. I love my life. I am safe. I love being loved. I love giving and receiving. I take in and utilize all of life's loving experiences.

## BREASTS

Your breasts represent nurturing of yourself and others. They also represent nourishment both physically, as in food, and emotionally, as in feelings. When one does not get enough nourishment either from others or from oneself, one may experience breast discomfort. When a woman does not enjoy being a nurturer, or finds herself nurturing others at her own expense, she may experience breast problems. Breasts also represent a woman's feelings about her own femininity and sensuality.

*Affirmations*

My breasts are beautiful. They are perfect just the way they are. I am balanced in giving and receiving love. I lovingly allow myself to be nurtured. I love to receive as much as I give.

## MIDRIFF

Your midriff represents how you deal with your emotions, with ease or difficulty, with confidence or fear. It holds your major secondary vital organs: your liver, spleen, kidneys, pancreas, the top of the large bowel, the top of the small bowel, stomach, duodenum, adrenal glands, and the top of the urethra. Each of these organs supports a different emotion, so you may say that your midriff stores or embraces your emotions. Extra weight around the midriff may indicate extra protection around your emotions. Soreness in the midriff area may indicate stressed emotions or the inability to process or cleanse negative emotions.

*Affirmations*

My midriff is perfect, strong, toned, smooth, and flexible. I am safe to feel all of my emotions. My emotions love me and allow me to experience life more fully with love and joy.

## WAIST

Your waist represents the ability to be flexible, to turn easily, and to see different angles and sides of life. It can show you how willing you are to change directions.

*Affirmations*

My waist is perfect, smooth, toned, strong, and flexible. I move with ease in my life, able to turn in any direction with joy and comfort.

## STOMACH (ABDOMEN)

Your abdomen houses your creativity and your "knowing" or gut reaction. When you experience problems such as stomach cramps or a building up of extra weight on the abdomen, there is a blockage in your life. You may be feeling trapped, stuck, or unable to move in or out of a certain situation. You may not be following your inner knowing. Or it may be a time of gestating new ideas, or waiting for the "right" moment. Discomfort in the abdomen may also be caused by fear that you are unable to move out of a certain situation. Fear is causing you to deny your self. Denial is the blockage causing the pain (or weight).

*Affirmations*

My stomach is beautiful, strong, and toned. It is perfect and I love it. I am safe to fully digest all that comes to me in my life. I am safe in every situation and with every new idea. It is okay for me to follow my inner knowing. I love my creativity.

## HIPS

Your hips and pelvis area represent balance, movement, and creativity. If you have problems in your hips, your life may be out of balance or you may be overloaded in one area (work versus play). It may also mean you are holding yourself back. And finally, your hips symbolize your relationship to your creativity or sexuality. If you have pain in your hips, you may want to look at how you are failing to express your uniqueness or how you may be denying your creativity or your sexuality.

*Affirmations*

My hips are perfect, strong, toned, shapely, and flexible. I am free to move forward, in perfect balance, with joy and laughter. There is joy in every day and in everything I do.

## BUTTOCKS

Your buttocks are the seat of power. When you have excess weight on the buttocks, it usually means fear of your own power. The buttocks hold the power that you are afraid of or unwilling to handle. When the buttocks are out of shape, power is mishandled or loosely held. It is particularly interesting that in this culture, large buttocks are more of a female problem than a male problem.

The buttocks are the center of all motion. When there is pain in the buttocks, power is blocked.

*Affirmations*

I love my buttocks. They are firm, toned, strong, and beautiful. I am safe in my power. I hold my power and use it wisely, and with love. I am safe in my power and with the power of others.

## THIGHS

Your thighs represent strength and forward motion. Excess weight on the thighs may mean you are holding on to the past or negative childhood memories associated with anger and rage. Very often if you cannot express anger, or you feel impotent in your anger, you may gain weight in your thighs. Pain in your thighs is also an expression of repressed anger and feelings of powerlessness.

*Affirmations*

My thighs are beautiful, strong, toned, and flexible. They move with grace and ease. I forgive all childhood trespasses, real and imagined, and go forth to positive feelings. I love life and enjoy my experiences, past and present.

## KNEES

Your knees represent balance, flexibility, pride, and ego. Pain or injury in the knee may mean there is an imbalance in your life. Look at the way you balance play in relation to work, or see whether your relationship is taking up all your energy at the expense of everything else in your life. Being inflexible in work, play, and relationships may also manifest in knee problems. Do you feel rigid or stuck, must you hold yourself at attention (accountable and therefore guilty before the fact), or are you at ease?

*Affirmations*

I love my knees. They are beautiful, strong, shapely, and flexible. My life is balanced. I work and play equally, with joy and delight. I bend and flow with ease.

## LOWER LEGS

Your lower legs represent carrying you forward in life. When there's pain, you may be stopping yourself. When there is extra weight, you may be weighing yourself down, and holding yourself back. The belief here is that you can't do it; therefore, you stop yourself.

*Affirmations*

I love my calves. They are beautiful, strong, toned, and well defined. I move forward in my life safely and with ease. I am safe now and in the future.

## ANKLES

As with the wrists, your ankles represent your ability to take in and receive pleasure. They also represent your ability to move with ease and flexibility. Ankles hold and protect your feelings of vulnerability (for example, the Achilles tendon). Additionally, ankles represent how quickly and comfortably you communicate (Mercury, the messenger of the Greek gods, has wings at his ankles).

*Affirmations*

I have beautiful ankles. They are strong, toned, and flexible. I am safe. I move with ease and flexibility and communicate freely. All is well with me in the world.

## FEET

Your feet are your base, your roots, your foundation. They represent understanding yourself and others. Pain in the feet is a great limiter and reflects a fear of going forward with freedom. Feet represent caring and taking time for yourself. In addition, they also represent following your own dreams. If you have pain in your feet, look to see where you are not nurturing yourself.

*Affirmations*

I love my feet. They are beautiful, strong, and flexible. I love my life and the way I choose to live. I am safe following my dreams. I love taking care of myself. All is well and perfect in my life.

## HEART

The heart represents the center of love and security.

*Affirmations*

My heart is strong. I am safe both giving and receiving love. I love myself and others. I am loved. I am secure.

## LUNGS

The lungs represent the ability to take in life.

*Affirmations*

My lungs are strong and healthy. I take in life fully and joyously. I love my life.

## BONES

Your bones represent structure. When you have bone problems, you may feel rebellious against the structure of society, your home life, or the way you have structured your life. Your life may be off track, so you stop yourself by breaking or bruising a bone.

*Affirmations*

My bones are strong. They carry me with strength and ease. I have perfect posture and look beautiful. My life is perfect. I love my life and the way I live it.

## SKIN

Your skin protects your individuality. Problems with your skin show a lack of belief in your own individuality or indicate you may feel invaded by others. Your skin is a sensor. When you have skin problems, you may be denying your senses, not allowing yourself to fully hear, see, feel, taste, or smell. Sensing also means allowing yourself to intuit situations. Skin problems may be the manifestation of your inability or unwillingness to follow your own sense of knowing.

*Affirmations*

I have perfect skin. It is beautiful, smooth, and toned. I love my skin. I am safe being me. I love myself and who I am. I enjoy the richness of life; I experience with delight my senses: hearing, seeing, feeling, tasting, and smelling. I trust my senses and know I am right.

## MUSCLES

Your muscles hold the whole structure of your life together. They allow you to move your structure. When muscles are sore, it may mean you are having difficulty moving within the structure of your life. Your life may be too structured, or you may not have enough structure.

*Affirmations*

I have strong, flexible, well-conditioned, well-toned muscles. They move with ease, strength, and fluidity. I love my beautiful muscles. I love my life and my freedom to move in any direction with ease and safety.

## SPECIFIC PROBLEMS

### CELLULITE

Cellulite represents stored anger, fear, and frustration. The body acts as a storage tank for unexpressed rage, disappointment, unhappiness, and frustration. It also stores unreleased fears. Cellulite is also a sign of self-denial and self-punishment. Somewhere, probably in childhood and then reinforced in relationships, you developed the belief that you are "wrong" or "not good enough" and you therefore need to be punished.

*Affirmations*

I love my body. I love the texture of my skin, the lines of my limbs, and the toned quality of every part of me. I live life joyously, happy with myself and with my experiences. I allow myself the joys and pleasures of life with delight. I am right in what I choose for myself. Life is a blessing and a joy. I release all fear (past and present) and go forth to beauty and joy.

## FAT

Fat represents fear. It is the body's way of protecting itself. Fat also can represent denial or fear of one's own feelings. The more overweight one becomes, the deeper the feelings are buried. Fat also may be a mechanism for covering over anger and disappointment.

*Affirmations*

I love my fat. It protects me and keeps me safe. It has done a great job and now it can go on vacation permanently. I am safe in every aspect and feeling in my life. I easily express and release my emotions with joy and in safety.

## FLEXIBILITY

The parts of your body that are inflexible reflect the way you are in relation to the world. The limitations of each of the major body areas is exacerbated by inflexibility; for example, tightness in the back of your legs may inhibit your going forward in your life. Tightness in the chest muscles may inhibit you in giving or receiving love. Tightness in the lower back may cause you to be locked into fear and almost always results in pain.

*Affirmations*

I am flexible. I move with grace and fluidity. I love the way I move. I love my life and all that it offers me. I enjoy new directions. Life is a joyous kaleidoscope of change.

## PAIN

Pain is an indication of self-punishment. Self-punishment is a response to guilt or fear. Guilt can stem from any cause, any childhood belief, or as a result of paying too much attention to your critical voice (or someone else's critical voice). Pain can be relieved as you release your feelings of guilt or fear.

*Affirmations*

My body feels great. I love my body; it loves me. I forgive myself for everything I have done, real or imagined, that I feel guilty about. I love myself and my way of being in the world. I release my fears and go forth to peace, prosperity, and happiness.

## STIFFNESS

Stiffness represents rigidity. It can manifest in simple muscle inflexibility or in sore and tight muscles. When you are unwilling to be flexible with ideas and beliefs, the body may become stiff, sore, and in extreme cases, spasms may occur.

*Affirmations*

My body moves with grace and ease. My muscles are flexible, well toned, and in good condition. I love new ideas. I am always open to new ideas and beliefs to enhance my life.

## SPASMS

Spasms represent tightening your thoughts through fear. When you are afraid to move forward, or afraid of the consequences, or just afraid, the muscles may spasm. Look at the area of your body that is experiencing the spasm and see whether your fear is related to whatever that part of the body represents.

*Affirmations*

My body feels good, relaxed, and in good condition. My muscles move with ease. They are fluid, strong, and relaxed. I am safe. It is a joy to be alive. I am okay just the way I am.

## POSTURE

Posture problems represent areas of your life that are out of alignment. Check where you have the posture problem and then look at that area of your life. How is it out of alignment? For example, round shoulders mean you are out of alignment in the way you are carrying your life's experiences. Do you feel constantly overburdened?

*Affirmations*

I have great posture. My body is beautiful, straight, and strong. It moves with grace and fluidity. I am perfect just the way I am. My life is joyous. I have what I want and feel good about myself. I love life.

# Foods

Nan Fuchs's book *The Nutrition Detective* has a wonderful chapter titled "The Anti-Illness Diet" that describes a healthy diet as one low in protein and fats and high in grains and legumes. Dairy products, animal protein, sugar, and caffeine are on the list of foods to avoid for healthy living. The following food categories are the ones to include in your diet in order of their importance and highest quantity:

Grains and legumes (peas and beans)

Vegetables

Protein

Fruit

Nuts and seeds

Fats and oils

I used to avoid many of these foods because they are regarded as fattening. Actually, while they are dense foods, most are actually low in fat and very filling. A little goes a long way.

## GRAINS AND LEGUMES

Grains and legumes in particular help balance blood sugar levels; they are high in fiber and provide bulk. Grains include:

| | |
|---|---|
| Barley | Oats (or oatmeal) |
| Brown rice | Rye |
| Buckwheat | Triticale |
| Cornmeal | Wheat (all forms) |
| Millet | |

They come in the form of whole grains, cracked grain, flakes, and flours. One of my favorites is to add about ¼ cup whole wheat groats to 1 cup brown rice and boil them up together. It makes the rice much chewier.

Legumes include:

| Peas (all kinds) | Beans | Lentils |
|---|---|---|
| black-eyed | azuki | Tofu |
| green | black | Peanuts |
| split | garbanzo | |
| | kidney | |
| | lima | |
| | mung | |
| | pinto | |
| | red | |
| | soy | |
| | white | |

## VEGETABLES

A vegetable diet is an anticonstipation diet because of the fiber and water it provides. Fresh vegetables are much better than frozen or canned. Canned vegetables in particular are overcooked and high in sodium. It's important to eat a wide variety of vegetables of all colors. The Weight Watchers diet is based on being able to eat all the vegetables you want (as long as they aren't served with lots of butter, sour cream, and sauces). Vegetables include:

| | |
|---|---|
| Alfalfa sprouts | Leeks |
| Artichokes | Lettuce (not iceberg) |
| Bean sprouts | Mushrooms |
| Beet greens | Okra |
| Beets | Onions |
| Bell peppers (green, red) | Parsley |
| Bok choy | Parsnips |
| Broccoli | Peas |
| Brussels sprouts | Potatoes |
| Cabbage | Radishes |
| Carrots | Snow peas |
| Cauliflower | Spinach |
| Celery | String beans/runner beans |
| Chinese cabbage | Summer squash |
| Collard greens | Sweet potatoes |

| | |
|---|---|
| Corn | Tomatoes |
| Crookneck squash | Turnip greens |
| Cucumbers | Turnips |
| Eggplant/aubergine | Winter squash |
| Jerusalem artichokes | Yams |
| Jicama | Zucchini/courgettes |

## PROTEINS

When we think proteins, we often think meat. In her book *Diet for a Small Planet*, Frances Moore Lappe promoted the concept of mixing legumes and grains to form whole proteins. Eating too many high-protein foods can trigger malabsorption problems and contribute to aging, cancer, atherosclerosis, and arthritis, to name a few. If you are going to cut down on protein, the protein you should reduce is animal. If you're going to eat animal protein, eat poultry without the skin, fish, and small amounts of low-fat or nonfat dairy products. Eggs should be eaten sparingly.

Grains, nuts, and seeds, when combined with beans and peas, will give you complete high-quality proteins. Soy milk, tofu, and soy-based protein powders are excellent alternatives.

## FRESH FRUIT

Whole fruit adds fiber to a diet and is an excellent intestinal cleanser. Fruit juices, by comparison, are higher in fructose, lower in fiber, and don't retain many of the vitamins and minerals that are stored just under the fruit's skin.

## NUTS AND SEEDS

Nuts and seeds are packed with protein and high in fats. They include:

| | |
|---|---|
| Almonds | Pine nuts |
| Brazil nuts | Pistachios (unsalted, undyed) |
| Cashews | Pumpkin seeds |
| Hazelnuts | Sesame seeds |
| Macadamia nuts | Sunflower seeds |
| Pecans | Walnuts |

Raw nuts and seeds in the shell remain fresh longest. Almonds are the lowest in fats.

## FATS AND OILS

Fats in small amounts are essential in the diet. Make certain the oil you use in cooking is a cold-pressed polyunsaturated vegetable oil such as:

| | |
|---|---|
| Canola | Safflower |
| Corn | Sesame |
| Olive | Soy |
| Peanut | Sunflower |

Like many Americans, I was raised on a diet high in animal protein. A meal without meat or dairy didn't seem like much of a meal. When all the new information came out about changing diets for healthy living, I began to experiment with vegetarian cooking and eating. It took a while to convince my palate, but, although I am not a vegetarian, I find I eat less and less animal protein and am beginning to prefer the lighter fare. And, although I still enjoy it, I find that I don't miss meat when it isn't served and mostly prefer a meatless dinner. Of great help in changing my palate were good cookbooks and good vegetarian diet books, as well as herbs, teas, and special vitamins. Listed below are some of my favorite books, plus a phone number for nutritional information from the company I use to advise me, Magic Chain. (I use the information these books impart in creating my own dishes. I am much too headstrong to follow someone else's program as if it were law.) Find what works for you and stay aware.

## Books

| | |
|---|---|
| *Diet for a New America* | John Robbins |
| *Diet for a Small Planet* | Frances Moore Lappe |
| *Fit for Life* | Harvey and Marilyn Diamond |
| *The Moosewood Cookbook* | Mollie Katzen |
| *The Nutrition Detective* | Nan Fuchs |
| *Reversing Heart Disease* | Dr. Dean Ornish |
| *The Vegetarian Epicure* | Anna Thomas |

## Products

Robert Green
Magic Chain
6965 El Camino Real
Suite 105
Rancho La Costa, CA 92009
(800) 622-6648

Enjoy your food, and be smart. Pay attention to what works for you and *tell the truth*.

For information on upcoming workshops and seminars, write MetaFitness, 513 Wilshire Blvd., Santa Monica, CA 90401, or call (310) 281-7744.